The HEART that SMILES

31 Day Challenge To Smile TOO for You

COLLEGE BOY
PUBLISHING
"We Breed Bestsellers"

SPRITUALITY/CHRISTIAN/SELF-HELP

Edited by **LaTangela Vann** & **Armani Valentino**
for College Boy Publishing, LLC

Published for print & digital distribution by **Armani Valentino**
Inside Designed & Setup by **Armani Valentino**
Cover Design by **Armani Valentino**

© 2017. SHELDA EVETTE.
All Rights Reserved.

No part of this book may be reproduced or transmitted in any form or by any means, electronic or mechanical, including photocopying, recording, or by any information storage and retrieval system, without permission in writing from the publisher.

Published in Dallas, TX, by College Boy Publishing. College Boy Publishing is a division of The College Boy Company & ArmaniValentino.com.

Copies of this book may be ordered directly from www.collegeboypublishing.com. Please allow up to 7-10 Business Days for delivery.

The author is available for keynote addresses, workshops, panel discussions, consultations, and radio & television interviews by emailing collegeboypublishing@gmail.com

Printed in the United States of America
08 09 10 11 12 MHAV 5 4 3 2 1

The HEART that SMILES

31 Day Challenge
To Smile TOO for You

By Shelda Evette

Foreword by Michele R. Wright, PhD

"A Joyful Heart
Makes A Cheerful Face,
But
When The Heart Is Sad,
The Spirit Is Broken."
~Proverbs 15:13~

CONTENTS

Letter Poem to the Reader

Foreword

Introduction

Day 1: You're Somebody's Reason to Smile
Day 2: Smiling Makes You Younger
Day 3: Your Smile Accessorizes Your Appearance
Day 4: Trouble Won't Last Always
Day 5: It's Time To Write A New Story
Day 6: Excellent Character Attracts Excellent Associations
Day 7: Think Superbly, Speak Superbly
Day 8: It's Always The Right Time To Love
Day 9: The Power Within
Day 10: The Source of Your Strength
Day 11: If You Can Move, You Can Grove
Day 12: Taking Steps Toward the Vision
Day 13: God Sees You As Royalty
Day 14: Forgiving As The Father
Day 15: Stepping Into Your Success Zone

CONTENTS

Day 16: Effective Communication

Day 17: Smell the Roses

Day 18: Building a Stronger You

Day 19: Desperation Begets Manifestation

Day 20: From Gossiper to Philosopher

Day 21: I Am Who I Show I Am

Day 22: Flaws Exist In All

Day 23: Praise the Creator

Day 24: Don't Lose Composure Over No Closure

Day 25: Having Whole Wisdom

Day 26: Pride Won't Be My Downside

Day 27: Lead Us Not Into Temptation

Day 28: Pray About Everything Everyday

Day 29: Plan. Prepare. Produce.

Day 30: Investing In Others

Day 31: Loving Yourself Completely

Letter to the Reader...

Dear Reader,

I wish to always see you complete and happy…wearing a radiant smile to compliment your beauty. Smile because you are amazing, captivating, and unique too. Smile from deep within, because no matter what, someone loves you. And you too, are that person's reason to smile…

The thought of you and your splendor makes it all worthwhile. We all have days to which the smile is used to cover up a multitude of tears… 'Tis easier to do—carry a smile that's untrue than face inevitable fears.

Always remember the power of the smile can trigger an unknown strength from inside you. And always remember, no matter the situation, obstacle, or circumstance—to flash your smile…

Just Because You Deserve To!

Yours Truly,

Shelda E.

Foreword

By
Michele R. Wright, PhD

As an Award-Winning Author, Inspirational Speaker, Success Expert, and Senior-Level Executive; I have been privy to a lot of amenities in life – some more costly than others. But as a Born-again, Baptized in Jesus Name, and Holy Ghost filled with the Evidence of Speaking in Tongues Christian, Daughter, and Woman of God; the most priceless things that I have attained in life is the "Gift" and the "Love" of God!!! This is why my heart is so full of Love, Admiration, Respect, and Reverence for God, my Lord and Savior Jesus Christ!!! "For in Him we live, and move, and have our being; as certain also of your own poets have said, For we are also His offspring" (Acts 17:28, KJV). And as two of His beloved offspring, Shelda Garland most eloquently and cleverly authors this life and heart-changing book, *The Heart That Smiles*, and I am most honored to Wright – write and right – this Foreword from my heart that smiles!

When Shelda first approached me about her long awaited project, I could not help but smile, because her smile is always so infectious. Interestingly, no matter how she is feeling or doing, I've never known her not to smile. She obviously realizes that there are a lot of things in life we cannot control, but we can choose to exhibit *"The Heart That Smiles"*. This is why it is essential to embrace God's instruction to "Count it all Joy…" (James 1:2, ESV). Who can resist a healthy, beautiful, inviting, irresistible, and contagious smile, which equates to a cheerful heart that smiles. And both the natural and spiritual fringe benefits are endless and priceless, including:

Ø "A cheerful look brings joy to the heart; good news makes for good health." ~ Proverbs 15:30, NLT

Ø "A cheerful heart is good medicine, but a broken spirit saps a person's strength."   ~ Proverbs 17:22, NLT

Ø "A glad heart makes a happy face; a broken heart crushes the spirit. A wise person is hungry for knowledge, while the fool feeds on trash. For the despondent, every day brings trouble; for the happy heart, life is a continual feast." ~ Proverbs 15:13-15, NLT

Ø "We were filled with laughter, and we sang for joy. And the other nations said, "What amazing things the Lord has done for them." Yes, the LORD has done amazing things for us! What joy!" ~ Psalms 126:2-3, NLT

Ø "Smile and watch God smile back at you!!!"
~ Dr. Michele R. Wright

What an unspeakable joy to know that everyday and without exception, we have so many reasons to smile in the Joy, Hope, Grace, Favor, Mercy, and Love of God. For Psalms 30:5, KJV, assures us, "For His anger endureth but a moment; in His favour is life: weeping may endure for a night, but joy cometh in the morning." So, regardless of your race, ethnicity, gender, socioeconomic background, personal issues, struggles, and justifiable yet often perceived excuses; we can all afford *The Heart That Smiles.*

A smile transcends languages, barriers, customs, and beliefs. For a smile needs no translation. It speaks for itself. And it costs absolutely nothing but a "Pure Heart" that is willing and desires to Smile, "For as he thinketh in his heart, so is he…" (Proverbs 23:7, KJV). So, what fuels the Heart? Simply Love!!! It must start and end with Love. Why is "Love" so Important?

1. Love is the Greatest Commandment of all. When Jesus was asked, "Teacher, which is the greatest commandment in the Law?" Jesus replied: " 'Love the Lord your God with all your heart and with all your soul and with all your mind.' This is the first and greatest commandment. And the second is like it: 'Love your neighbor as yourself.' ~ Matthew 22:36-39, NIV

2. "Whoever does not love does not know God, because GOD IS LOVE." ~ 1 John 4:8, KJV

3. "In the beginning was the Word, and the Word was with God, and the Word was God." ~ John 1:1, KJV

4. "And now these three remain: Faith, Hope and Love. But the greatest of these Is Love."

~ 1 Corinthians 13:12, NIV

In reality, one's Faith can leave you, your Hope can forsake you, but Love (God ~ Jesus Christ) will never leave you nor forsake you (for The Living Bible tells us so). Even the late songstress Whitney Houston proclaimed, "Love is the Greatest Gift of all". What an irrefutable reason for *"The Heart That Smiles"*. And if that's not enough in itself, here's another indisputable cause, "For God so loved the world, that He gave His only begotten Son, that whosoever believeth in Him should not perish, but have everlasting life" (John 3:16, KJV).

God's Love and the Love of Jesus Christ give us all infinite and heartfelt reasons to Smile. And as we continue our journey towards *"The Heart That Smiles"*, let us wholeheartedly, "Be joyful in hope, patient in affliction, faithful in prayer" (Romans 12:12, NIV). And dare not forget, the Best in Christ, Love, Life, Heart, and Smiles is still yet to come!!! God Bless you and keep you as we all continue spreading the Love and *The Heart That Smiles!*

Sincerely written with *"The Heart That Smiles,"*

Michele R. Wright, Ph. D.

A Servant after God's Own Heart

Author, "DEAR SUCCESS SEEKER: *Wisdom From Outstanding Women*"

Introduction

Our smiles have constructive power. They can inspire us to get motivated, excited, or simply to smile back at others. Whenever we see someone smiling, most of us immediately connect that person's smile to a joyful moment in their life. So, is this to say that someone who always smiles is always joyful? Not at all—our smiles can also be used to cover up our true emotional identity.

Have you ever wondered how a smile is connected to the heart, and if the impact a genuine or forced smile has on the heart matters? A genuine smile lights the eyes up and reflects true happiness from the heart, while a forced smile reflects an awkward look on the face. Within the heart can lie a range of emotions including joy, anger, loneliness, happiness, sadness, and so on. These emotions have a direct effect on the heart, and it shows throughout the body from the organs within to the smile shown outwardly. The Bible tells us in Proverbs 15:13 that a joyful heart makes a cheerful face, but when the heart is sad, the spirit is broken (NASB).

The heart is more than a pump distributing oxygenated blood throughout your body. The heart is also a sophisticated command center connecting and regulating all your organs. With each heartbeat, the heart plays a pivotal role in transferring information and connecting the intellect, the emotions, and the body. The energies available through the heart can be used to transform your experience at the physical, emotional, mental, and spiritual levels. (According to youareenergy.com/heart_smiling.html)

Almost everyone has experienced some of the heart's superior emotions like appreciation, joy, compassion, understanding, love, etc. These emotions can trigger a smile from the heart. But what does it mean when the heart can no longer produce the energy to engage such emotions? What causes the heart to stop smiling? Of the many diverse reasons a person ceases to smile from the heart, I personally know one--depression. Research has shown that depression is one of the human race's most common and distressing afflictions, disrupting the lives of an estimated 300 million individuals worldwide.

I was depressed for over 12 years, but no one knew because I was always smiling. Although my heart had stopped smiling, I was able to force a smile that came across to others as though I was so happy and energetic. So, how was I able to fool so many people for so many years? I mean, most depressed people stay in bed for most of the day, are sad or angry, and stay clear of social events, right?

Well, I was definitely depressed, but I was also able to function...thus comes the term "functional depression." I have always worked in a career that involves association with administrators, students, and the community. I got out of bed every day and reported to work on time appearing to be as happy as I could be. I put a bright smile on my face and engaged with co-workers as needed. I attended family and social functions but would often cite an excuse to leave the event early. I did what I needed to get by in the public eye, but behind closed doors my energy levels were low. I seemed hopeless. I had so many regrets. Life for me had become more about surviving than thriving.

Today, I am no longer "functionally depressed." I have moments of despair but they are just that—for a moment. Today, I have a heart that smiles and triggers an amazing energy that radiates genuine joy on my face. So, what made my heart smile again? It was repentance, acceptance, and appreciation. I repented of living life in my own strength and through my own understanding...and choosing to dwell in a place of despair for so long. I accepted that God loves me so much that He brought me into a world of abundance to enjoy with purpose. I appreciate my purpose to live a fulfilled life for God through loving, serving, and praising Him for all of His majesty. Now I have an inward joy that causes my heart to smile.

You deserve a heart that smiles too. Sometimes life gives us a million reasons to break down, cry, and stay in a place of despair, but we must reflect on the million reasons we have to smile and push forward. In this book, you have the opportunity to journal 31 experiences that make you smile, so when incidents occur to steal your joy, you can reflect back on those things that give you joy. You can live your life successfully with joy no matter who you are, where you are, or what you have.

I wrote this book of 31 reasons that make me

smile in hopes that you will be blessed and inspired to discover 31 reasons or more you can, "Smile Too For You."

The HEART that SMILES

I Smile Because...

I AM SOMEONE'S REASON TO SMILE

DAY 1

According as He hath chosen us in Him before the foundation of the world, that we should be holy and without blame before Him in love.

Ephesians 1:4

You're Somebody's Reason to Smile

    You don't have to be the most hilarious person to make others smile…just being you and just doing you has an effect on others. However, the secret is being able to make yourself smile first…being happy with you and the things that you do. Maya Angelou made this clear when she said, "Success is liking yourself, liking

The Heart That Smiles

what you do, and liking how you do it." Be you! Someone, somewhere is happy—very happy to know you, and when your name races across their mind, they smile.

Growing up, I used to cite the phrase, "Smile, Jesus loves you," to whomever I thought was feeling sad. As I got older, this phrase helped me get through some lonesome times. Loneliness is a real emotion. We may feel lonely, even when we're not alone. Most of us have a desire to feel connected in some way, and when we're not, we may experience an emptiness. And this emptiness may lead to a sense of having no worth.

When my marriage of 16 years ended with divorce, I went through the same emotional stages of someone who had lost a loved one to death. Even if others try to convince you that God interceded to bring the marriage to an end, you may still find yourself trying to hang on to what's gone. It's really tough to let go of someone when you have been around that person for a significant amount of time, especially if that person is all you've known on that level.

For me, the stage of loneliness seemed never ending. Marriage was everything to me. I took it serious and was faithful in it. I thought I would be with this man forever. Having a partner to share life with meant the world to me. I just could not imagine starting over with someone else. Along with the loneliness came

DAY 1

feelings of worthlessness. I went day by day trying to survive. I disconnected myself from family and friends, and connected myself to a failed relationship. I heard whispers of people thinking I would end up taking my life. The devil is a lie. I can't deny that it hurt me to the core, but I also could not deny my four precious little ones the rest of my life. It was their constant hugging, loving, them wanting to be around me, and my yearning desire to be delivered that finally snapped me out my trance of loneliness. Like it was for me, there will always be others who still see your true value after a demeaning experience. I learned to stop allowing my painful circumstances to depreciate my worth and instead, allowed them to grow my worth.

I realized that I had a right to be and walk in all that God has destined for me. I had been stuck in my comfort zone for way too long. I had shut down from past hurt, with low self-esteem and resentment. I wasn't speaking up against things I knew were wrong; instead, I was avoiding things so I wouldn't have to face an altercation or argument because they were draining.

Even though there are times when you may feel lonely and insignificant, it is at these very moments that you must remember that you are important and you matter. You were planned to be here. You were chosen… Jesus chose you! He hand-picked and appointed you for a specific purpose that only you can fulfill. And when you are walking in your purpose, not only for you but for others as well—it should make your heart smile!

I smiled today because/when...

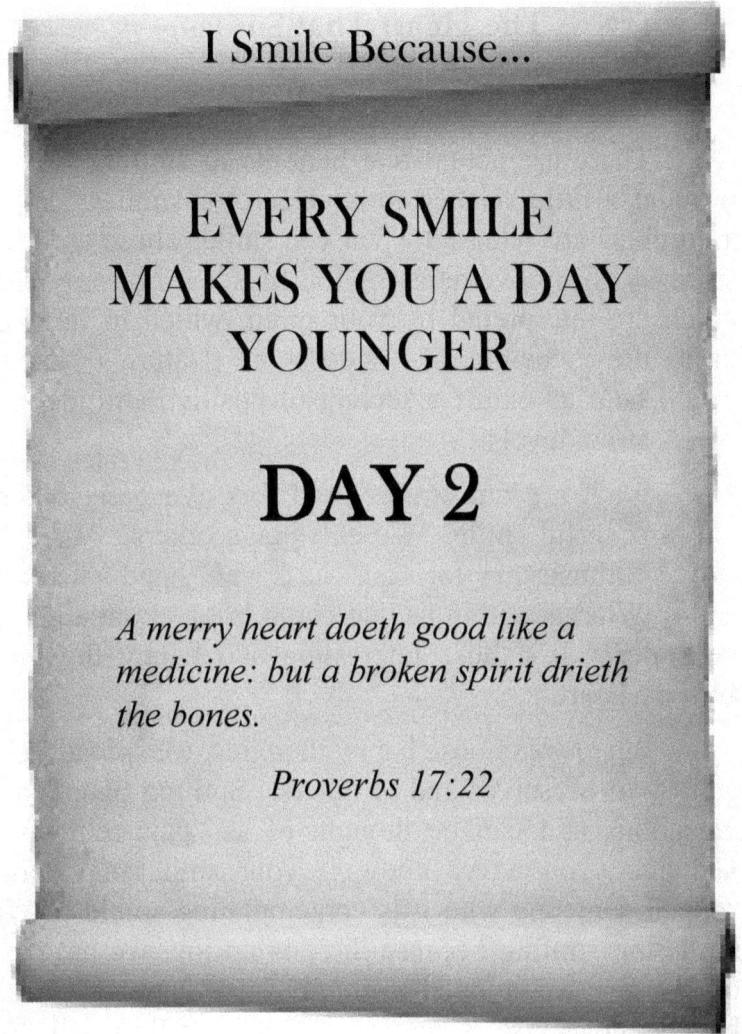

Smiling Makes You Younger

    Do you know someone who looks much older than they really are? I'm sure several factors may have contributed to their premature aging, but I can't help but wonder how often they smile.

The Heart That Smiles

There are actual real benefits to smiling. Let's consider a little science first. Neurotransmitters called endorphins are released when you smile. These are triggered by the movements of the muscles in your face, which are interpreted by your brain, which in turn releases these chemicals. Endorphins (Nature's "happy drug") help us exude a feeling of positive attitude and lowers stress levels.

What are our smiles used for? We greet others with a cheerful smile. We encourage others. We also show enthusiasm for our task at hand with a smile. What is within us that could bring about a genuine smile? It's those interesting and happy thoughts from the heart.

When we choose happy thoughts, we spread light and joy to ourselves and to others. Smiling people are contagious and can be thought of as "pain-relieving" medicine…you never know if your smile may have stopped someone who was contemplating suicide. We don't stop smiling because there is no joy; we have no joy because we stopped smiling. What happens in life that would cause someone to stop smiling all together? Constant stress at work, the state of the country, or just getting old in general are some contributors.

For Jamie, it was being laid off late in his career and unable to find other work. This put him in a financial crisis. Money problems are among the top reasons a person may stop smiling. It's certainly nothing joyful

DAY 2

about not being able to pay your bills. However, Jamie was only 42 but looked like he was 62, because he was always worrying about his future. He allowed his situation of not having enough money to monopolize his thoughts. It took his sister to show him that he was not living his life because he was too consumed with worrying about it. Jamie's sister felt that if he wasn't living, he was dying, and she could not just stand by and watch him die. She knew how much her brother loved to make outdoor furniture, so she reminded him of the bench he had promised to build for her, now that he had the time. Jamie was very happy for the challenge, and his sister was very happy the challenge was forcing him to live.

I smiled today because/when...

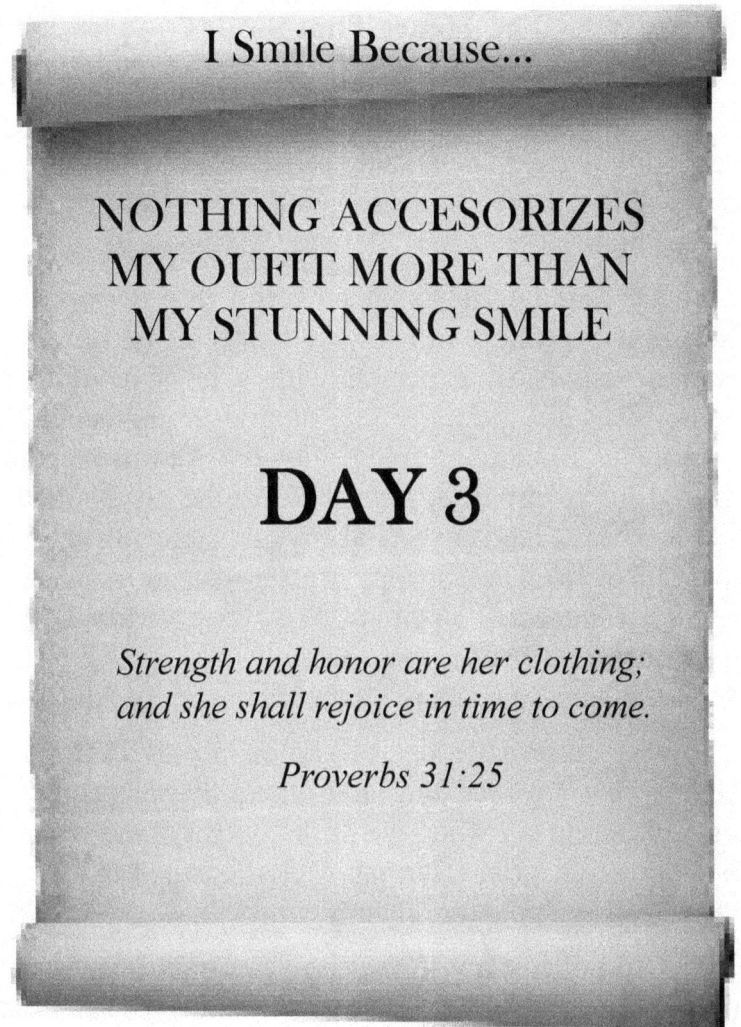

Your Smile Accessorizes Your Appearance

You're looking in the mirror saying to yourself, "Wow...I look amazing," with a slight smirk on your face. The first compliment you receive, that smirk turns into a smile, as to say, "I agree." Does this make you arrogant or cocky? Neither. That makes you confident, and confidence is important.

The Heart That Smiles

Our confidence begins with self-esteem which is the core emotional need of every human being, and we want it to be high.

A single smile is so powerful that it can often transform a person with low self-esteem, jolting them from negativity to a person with a positive attitude. Conley was the best dressed supervisor in the building…that is from his shoulders down. Not many people noticed his extravagant attire because he always had a frown on his face and was always irritable. Instead of being recognized as a snappy dresser, he was recognized as just being plain snappy. We were always telling crack-me-up jokes in hopes that he would crack a smile. He had a talent of sucking all the air out the building.

We wear a variety of smiles in our lifetimes—some which are revealing and others that are concealing. We smile big when we have a victory, and we grin to suppress chagrin. Herman Melville called the smile, "the chosen vehicle for all ambiguities."

And one of my former bosses would say, "When in doubt, wear a smile…no one will know you're clueless." One of my favorite smiles to wear, is the "love smile." I wear it around everyone…family, friends, and strangers too. It's that smile that's so contagious.

The next time you walk into that interview, meeting, gym, etc.—walk in wearing a genuine smile to greet others. Smiling may help you appear approachable and is linked to a happier life with more success.

I smiled today because/when...

I smiled today because/when...

_____
_____
_____
_____
_____
_____
_____
_____
_____
_____
_____
_____
_____
_____
_____
_____
_____
_____
_____
_____
_____
_____
_____
_____
_____
_____

I Smile Because...

THE DAY TROUBLE COMES, IT WON'T LAST ALWAYS

DAY 4

For our light affliction, which is but for a moment, worketh for us far more exceeding and eternal weight of glory.

2 Corinthians 4:17

Trouble Won't Last Always

There is a purpose why we suffer, whether it is to make us stronger or just mindful that none of us are exempt from trouble. However, we should not allow our troubles to diminish our faith or even disillusion us. A difficult divorce after 18 years brought my friend to this revelation.

The Heart That Smiles

The resolution of her marriage left her in an emotional, physical, spiritual, mental, and financial mess. Even though her marriage was unhealthy, she fought for it. She gave her all, and her husband gave up. He refused family counseling and anger management time after time. Eventually, my friend gave up... she had no more fight in her. Forced to move out of their five bedroom home into a three bedroom apartment within a matter of one week, had her beyond frazzled.

When she got divorced, my friend was a stay at home mom and property manager for their rental properties, and her husband was a captain in the army. She was given custody of their three children. Her husband was able to hire an attorney, who managed to prevent him from paying any alimony because of her ability to earn a good income based on her level of education and very little in child support. She was jobless and barely making rent; her car was repossessed, oldest child acting out, and she felt like she was about to lose her mind.

Her husband received all proceeds from their rental properties in his personal account during the marriage, and he continued to do so after the divorce. One of the properties was being financed, and instead of paying the mortgage, he pocketed the rent money. This added even more insult to my friend's credit. She was in despair. Her ex-husband remarried three months after their divorce. He then began to take my friend back and forth to court over silly stuff--just because he could. All

DAY 4

that this experience entailed sent my friend into an extended pity party. She was over a thousand miles away from her home in Texas--stuck in New York with no friends and no family. She felt as if she was down to nothing, and this went on for several months.

She shared with me how one Saturday night, she went into her 6 X 6 closet, curled up, and began to really cry out to God. She pleaded Him to bring an end to her troubles. In deep distress she prayed, "Help me, Lord, to hold on. I am so tired…this is all too much to deal with. I know you see my struggles, but why won't You help me, Lord? I am so hurt, disappointed, and alone. I never imagined raising my children on my own. Please send me some help, a job, transportation, and peace."

The next morning she and her children accepted an invitation from her neighbor and went to a church. The Pastor had just begun preaching a 7 week sermon on, "Lessons from Job's Suffering." There were days she didn't want to get out of bed, but she kept pushing and made it to every sermon.

Many of us are familiar with the story of Job. How he suffered through great loss, devastation, and physical illness. This faithful and righteous man of God literally lost everything. His suffering and tragedy was so great that even his own wife said, "Are you still holding on to your integrity? Curse God and die!" Although Job maintained his faithfulness to God throughout his life, he still struggled deeply through the

The Heart That Smiles

trenches of pain. My friend shared how she could relate to how Job felt when he cried out to God, asking why did he not perish at birth, and die as he came from the womb (Job 3:11). She could relate when Job cried out that he had no peace, no quietness, no rest, but only turmoil (Job 3:26). Job loathed his very life, and gave free rein to his complaint and spoke out in the bitterness of his soul (Job 10:1). When he cried out that terrors overwhelm him...his life ebbs away, days of suffering grip him; the night pierces his bones, and his growing pains never rest (Job 30:15-17), Na'Kenya could relate. Like Job, my friend too, was in a very dark place. She was wallowing in self-pity.

Na'Kenya had associated herself with every failed event that had occurred in her life. This sent her into an extended self-pity party. She felt as though she had a right to be upset. She wanted others to see how unfair it was that all these bad things had happened to her. While listening to the sermons, she realized how she was only one step away from self-righteousness because she had begun to keep track of all her life's injustices. Na'Kenya shared how one Sunday the pastor encouraged the congregation to start looking at life's trials as a means for development and refinement. To ask oneself, "What can I learn and how can I grow from this?" rather than, "Who did this to me and how can I get out of it?" When the pastor went on to say that the trials were only temporary, my friend said tears began to roll down her face as this was the most joyful news she

DAY 4

had ever heard. My friend realized that she had lost a lot of ground while she was wallowing in her sorrows. She left church that day with new convictions about herself and her circumstances. She stopped complaining, moping, and groping and replaced all of that with words and actions of life. Na'Kenya began to speak things like, "Father God, I acknowledge my way is not working. I surrender it all to You, and I can't wait to see how You turn all of this around."

My friend stopped isolating herself and opened up to the mentors and divine connections God sent. Her prayer life began to change. She was inspired by how Job's sincere prayer for his friends led to his deliverance and his restoration. My friend forgave and began praying for those who had hurt her, lied on her, and schemed against her. She started standing on God's promises and speaking His Word over her life for a covering and for protection. My friend began expecting restoration.

By week four, a member of the church who had been watching her dedication and determination, offered her a job as an administrative assistant for her new Speech Therapy company. The salary was more than she had expected. By the end of week seven, her life had already begun to turn around. She started paying off old debts; loving herself again; she lost weight and was looking amazing. Almost three years from the date of her divorce, Na'Kenya published her first book, and it went on to become a best-seller.

The Heart That Smiles

She also became a renowned speaker and motivator. She has empowered many to be just as extraordinary as she. And that's not it… she crossed paths with a friend that had a crush on her in high school, 20 years later. He is a radio host and was the first person to interview her, helping to launch her book. Today, they are happily married, and he treats her like the queen she has always been and loves her children as if they were his own.

This may sound like a fairy tale, but it's not. It is the story of a woman who was suffering, found enough strength to take one step, and then watched God do the rest by opening up doors that once seemed impossible. Her troubles turned into opportunities! Her heart smiled again!

I smiled today because/when...

Do You Remember Me?

It's me, Lord standing in the need of prayer
It's me, Lord standing while broken in despair
It's me, Lord. Here I am. Can You not see me?
I'm far from my life I believe You destined it to be
It's me, Lord. Here I am. Can You not hear me crying?
I keep praying for a breakthrough that will reverse my soul from dying...

Forgive me, O Lord, for my temper tantrum. You see...
I went to that place of doubt, but it's only temporary
You are mighty, victorious, and so much bigger than all of this
These overwhelming circumstances--You, O Lord, have the power to dismiss
So I'll keep trusting, praising, and believing You alone
I'll keep my eyes focused on the One who sits on the throne

It's me, Lord standing in the days of my latter
It's me, Lord standing so much greater than my former
It's me, Lord...Your daughter, Shelda, who unto You--all her worries rendered
It's me, Lord...Your daughter, Shelda, who You have always loved and have remembered!

By: Your Child… *Shelda Evette*

I Smile Because...

I HAVE A NEW STORY TO WRITE, AND IT LOOKS NOTHING LIKE MY PAST

DAY 5

Brethren, I count not myself to have apprehended: but this one thing I do, forgetting those things which are behind, and reaching forth unto those things which are before.

Philippians 3:13

It's Time To Write a New Story

    Have you ever heard someone say, "I am so glad I don't look anything like what I've been through?" For years, you may find yourself repeating the same cycle within your career, your relationships, your health and

The Heart That Smiles

life in general. And then... one day, you decide you've had enough and want a change. You begin a new book of your life that is not a sequel to any past stories.

Not a day went by that Sharla did not complain about something. One day it was her kids, and the next day it was her husband (the bulk of her complaints). Then it may be her car or her weight. It was always something. It was obvious she was hurting over some incident, but the way she kept resurrecting her hurt and pain wasn't solving anything. Furthermore, the workplace was not the place to receive the type of counseling she obviously needed. My interaction with her would often include dialogue of encouraging phrases like, "I'm sorry that happened to you...pray and it will get better." I'm sorry...I know we all have issues we need to vent about, but hearing complaints every single day gets old and distressing, especially when you are trying to be more positive about your own issues. It was only in due time that someone would be transparent with her. That was Kim...she let Sharla have it, and the entire second floor heard it.

"Sharla, you really need to shut-up...you make it so hard to concentrate and be productive! Just leave your husband already...he probably wants to leave you!" That was the gist of what Kim shouted to Sharla. One would have expected Sharla to respond in defense; instead, her eyes filled with tears as she walked away toward the restrooms. Unfortunately, it took that outrageous episode for Sharla to examine herself. Not

DAY 5

only did she stop complaining about her personal life around the office, but when asked how she and her family were doing, she would reply with a constructive response, "We're blessed."

It was obvious that Sharla had a new conviction about herself. Her speech had changed from speaking death over her situations to speaking life over them. I was so proud of her...she had become a different person for the better, and for the remainder of the time I worked with her...she did not revert to her old ways. Hallelujah!

I smiled today because/when...

I Smile Because...

MY CHARACTER EXUDES EXCELLENCE, AND I ATTRACT WONDERFUL, SUCCESSFUL PEOPLE TO MY LIFE

DAY 6

Blessed is the man that walketh not in the counsel of the ungodly, nor standeth in the way of sinners, nor sitteth in the seat of the scornful.

Psalms 1:1

<u>Excellent Character Attracts Excellent Associations</u>

Many of us want friends or associations with some kind of status…the ones that are smart, funny, successful, etc. Oftentimes, what we want in our friends may be different from who we are.

The Heart That Smiles

When you start to notice that your friends are having a negative impact on your character, and you're not liking the people you keep attracting—it's time to be DIFFERENT. You want a wonderful friend—Be Wonderful. A wonderful person usually possesses a myriad of great characteristics such as kindness, patience, and even great humor. Be the change you want to attract!

I am constantly telling my children to be mindful of their associations. Friends and acquaintances can have a profound influence on us, and often in very subtle ways. My oldest son was easily influenced and often made behavior choices that were in the majority.

Proverbs 13:20 says, "Walk with the wise and become wise, for a companion of fools suffers harm." Those who don't benefit you by imparting wisdom, will hurt you by leading or advising you to do something foolish. I do my best to give Godly advice to others which attracts company with those who also give and show Godly wisdom.

We all have different ways we may define success; however, there should be a common thread for all: Being the best you can; Doing the best you can; Liking you, what you do, and how you do it.

I smiled today because/when...

I smiled today because/when...

I Smile Because...

I CHOOSE TO SPEAK SUPERBLY OF MYSELF AND MY SITUATION

DAY 7

For as he thinketh in his heart, so is he...

Proverbs 23:7

Think Superbly, Speak Superbly

    The only opinions of SELF that truly matters are our own. When we believe in ourselves, so do others. We are as our thoughts. We have control over our thoughts—to think negatively or to think positively. The same applies to our actions. We can choose to do what is right or what is wrong…what is acceptable or what is unacceptable.

The Heart That Smiles

As I reflect back on the infamous childhood idiom, "Sticks and stones may break my bones, but words can never hurt me," I can't think of any other phrase that so blatantly denies the power of words. I remember a time when a friend was in a very dark place in her life. So much so, she tried to take her life. Her significant other, at the time, realized what she had done and took her to the emergency room. The ride there was one she hasn't been able to forget. Her husband yelled, "How are we going to make the car payment now that you are increasing our expenses with this hospital bill you are about to make?" Perhaps he was acting out, in anger, because of what she had done. She shared with me that she could not have felt any lower. For years, this resonated with her as if her life was being compared to a car payment. Make no mistake about it, words can hurt, maim, wound, and devastate.

On the other hand, words can also build, transform, heal, touch, and bring hope. Over the years, I have become an expert at encouraging myself. I use catchy, poetic phrases. When I find myself feeling fearful of a project or speech to be presented…I tell myself, "I'm gonna rock the room with a boom, boom." Or when I find myself feeling unworthy…I say, "I'm worth it, and that's legit." And when I'm faced with unwanted circumstances…I say, "All is well and I will prevail." These jazzy little phrases always make me smile and help calm me; thus making me confident, relaxed, and ready to conquer any task set before me.

DAY 7

When I felt that I was always misunderstood, I began to journal my thoughts and feelings for cathartic release. One day, I read over 30 past journal entries, and noticed, with great satisfaction, the new conviction and growth that had occurred. One of the latter entries was a poem titled, *Beyond the Image:*

Looking in the mirror, what do I see?

I see a vivacious yet gracious woman looking at me!

Looking in the mirror, what do I see?

I see a gentle, calm spirit looking at me!

Looking in the mirror, what do I see?

I see an eager and motivated soul looking at me!

Looking in the mirror, what do I see?

I see an intelligent, imaginative, and yes!...inquisitive mind looking at me!

Looking in the mirror, what do I see?

I see a woman of great success and amazing beauty,

And for the first time, I'm looking at Me!

I've had several people say to me, "I want to speak more positively, but I don't know what to say." If you can relate and are feeling stuck because of positive "word blocks," write your name in the rectangular box on the next page and have your way with over 150 superb words to speak over yourself.

The Heart That Smiles

Abundant Believer Impressive

Principled Stunning Carefree Faithful Spiritual Prominent Intuitive

Zesty Giving Friendly Superb Vivacious

Visionary Receiver Lively Lovely Admirable Smiling Genius

Divine Delightful Upstanding Special Energetic Polished Remarkable

Upbeat Optimistic Phenomenal Bright Beautiful Handsome Stupendous Noble Memorable

Prudent Valuable Positive Poised Optimistic Kind Graceful Perseverance Celebrated

Growing Glowing Royalty Legendary Wise Exquisite Distinguished Legacy Gratifying

Sunny Strong Great Protected Wonderful Innovative Patient Lofty Resplendent

Festive Understanding Genuine Blessed Covered Unity Empathetic Humble

Plentiful Dazzling Fun Humorous Anointed

Day 7

Excellent Super Laughter

Lucid Young-At-Heart Playful Admirable Pretty Sparkling Adventurous

Good Active Inspirational Supportive Encouraging

Productive Helpful Humility

Joyful Thankful Prepared Terrific Thriving Fantastic Prayerful Caring

Fulfilled Spontaneous Marvelous Wondrous Fabulous Grateful Modest Whimsical

Intellectual Happy Worthy Beaming Radiant Unique Chosen

Disciplined Peaceful Gentle Generous Warrior Victorious Mighty Glamorous Enlarged

Restored Elevated Vindicated Delivered Rescued

Defended Refreshed Glorious Brilliant Eminent

Renowned Splendid Shining Triumphant Gorgeous

Amazing Adored Esteemed Grand

I smiled today because/when...

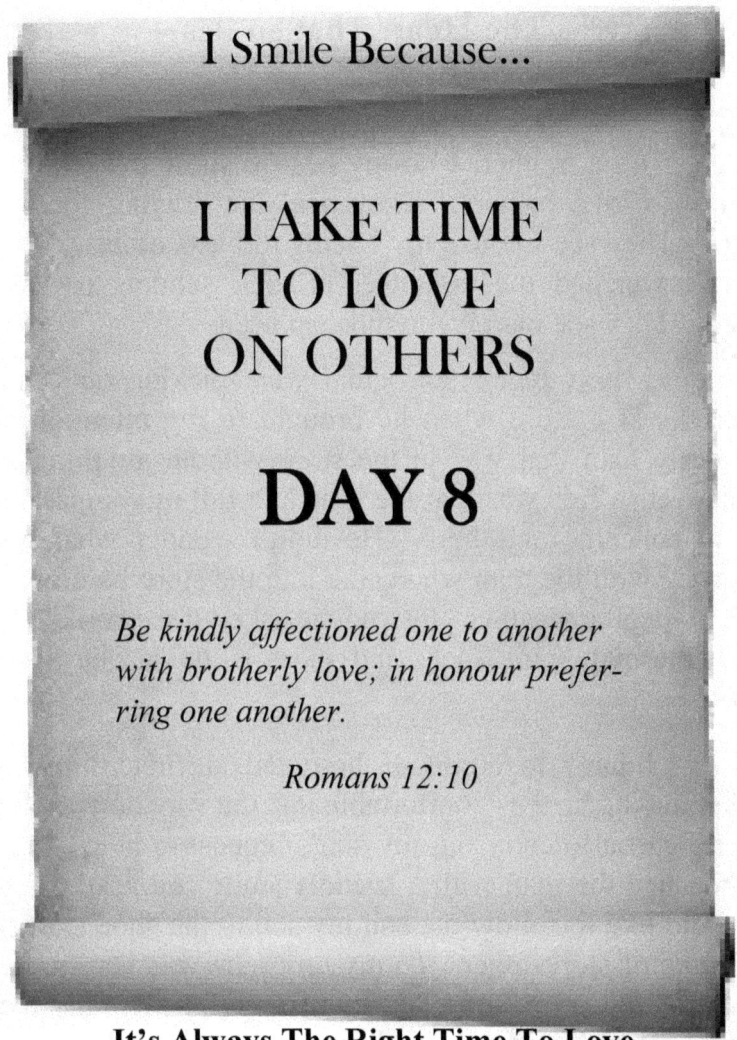

I Smile Because...

I TAKE TIME TO LOVE ON OTHERS

DAY 8

Be kindly affectioned one to another with brotherly love; in honour preferring one another.

Romans 12:10

It's Always The Right Time To Love

     Love has no limits. It can be expressed by doing several acts of kindness like serving, hugging, instructing, disciplining, caring, feeding the homeless, and so much more. When you are fluent in the language of love--kindness, compassion, and the desire to serve--flow from within you.

The Heart That Smiles

As a mother, I do my best to show my children how to love others. They hear me praying for others. They see me use my talents to bless others. They have watched me volunteer at their schools or shelters. They see me give to those in need.

My youngest son and I were picking out some snacks at a store when he brought to my attention an elderly man that was in the store without anything on his feet. Chris was 8 at the time and full of compassion and concern for others. He didn't wonder what was wrong with the man who came into the store barefooted in 30 degree weather. Instead, he asked if we could help get the man some socks and shoes so he can be warm too.

I have to admit…I hesitated at first…thinking that maybe he was comfortable just the way he was, but later chose to carry out my son's request to help. I approached the man with a friendly smile and asked if he would like to follow me and my son to the shoe store, a couple of stores over. To my relief, he was very grateful for the offer and even more grateful after his feet were covered. My son and I walked away smiling from the heart because we felt blessed that we were able to be a blessing to someone else.

DAY 8

Let Humanity Arise

The concept of humanity for Dr. King was defined in one of his most profound quotes, "Make a career of humanity, Commit yourself to the noble struggle for equal rights. You will make a greater individual of yourself, a greater nation of your country, and a finer world to live in."

Humanity to Dr. King was living your life selflessly and with love for everyone. It's dedicating yourself to fairly help others meet their needs until the service is completely done.

When I see the homeless on a cold, rainy day under a bridge for shelter,
I pull over, reach into the trunk of my car, and grab them some warm cover.

I Am Humanity!

The Heart That Smiles

When you see a family standing together with signs asking for help with basic necessities, you stop, reach into your wallet, and give a donation toward their needs.

You Are Humanity!

No matter what our talents are, we use them in some fashion to make this world the best it can be! Whether a student, doctor, parent, teacher, entertainer, or more—We dedicate ourselves to helping others.

We Are Humanity!

Let Humanity Arise!

I smiled today because/when...

I smiled today because/when...

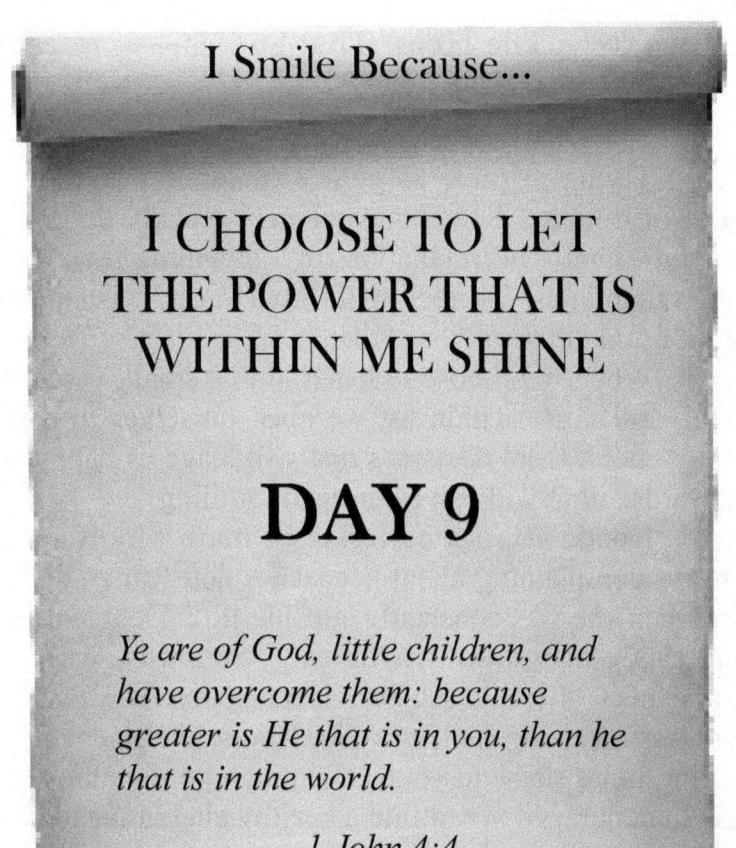

The Power Within

Most of us have been in predicaments that are either overwhelming or tempting. Our flesh gets weak at times due to stress, burdens, etc. This can cause us to become vulnerable to temptation, fear, and even depression.

The Heart That Smiles

Trying to shine on your own can get you into a heap of trouble. Sometimes we may quickly do or say hurtful things in retaliation to something that hurt us. Oftentimes, we feel awful afterwards, wishing we hadn't said "this" or done "that."

When we choose to listen to that small, yet powerful, still voice within us, we open ourselves to make better choices and decisions that will leave us happy afterwards…that will leave our hearts smiling.

I once asked a coworker of mine why was she always complaining about headaches and fear of diabetes when she was constantly stuffing little Debbie cakes and candy bars down her throat. "Seriously, what do you expect," I would ask her. Her response was that the job was stressing her out. So, I was like, but you're adding more stress to yourself through your eating habits. I encouraged her to find a healthy alternative to deal with the stresses of the job. I suggested she squeeze a stress ball, chew gum, or even chump on something with natural sugars like strawberries and grapes; most importantly, I encouraged her to pray and ask God to take her habit away. It took a while, but she eventually started making better choices, and thus became more pleasant to be around.

I smiled today because/when...

I smiled today because/when...

I Smile Because...

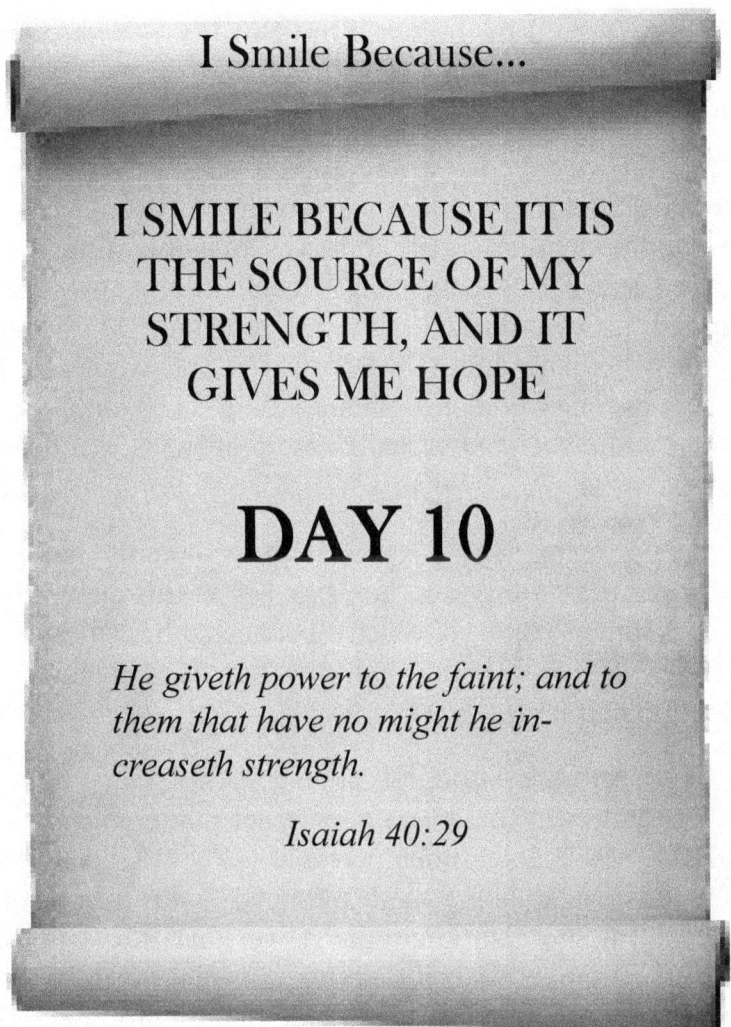

I SMILE BECAUSE IT IS THE SOURCE OF MY STRENGTH, AND IT GIVES ME HOPE

DAY 10

He giveth power to the faint; and to them that have no might he increaseth strength.

Isaiah 40:29

The Source of Your Strength

"Sometimes your joy is the source of your smile, but sometimes your smile can be the source of your joy" (Thich Nhat Hanh). With the simple act of a smile, you can release tension and gain the strength to turn your situation from gory to glory.

The Heart That Smiles

When asked, "Where do you get your sweet personality from," I would always respond with, "My paternal grandmother." Grandma Cat was one of the most loving and caring persons you could ever know. She smiled her way through almost everything. She would smile when she didn't feel so well. She would smile when she answered the phone. And she would even smile while she was verbally disciplining us grandchildren.

Growing up, I associated Grandma's smiling with her personality and just saw her as this super nice grandmother. As I got older, I connected her smiling to her joy and her hope, and saw her as a woman of strength and faith.

Even the strongest people grow weary sometimes, and even the nicest people get intolerable sometimes. My grandmother personally knew God as the source of her being and ultimately was strong in Him. But she also knew the power that lies within a smile and tapped into it daily as a means to renew her strength. Grandma Cat was clothed with vigor and dignity. She lived a life helping others, caring for others, and being the best blessing that she could be to others. Grandma Cat left this world smiling from her heart.

I smiled today because/when...

I smiled today because/when...

I Smile Because...

GOOD THINGS ARE HAPPENING TO ME TODAY...

I WOKE UP WITH THE ABILITY TO MOVE

DAY 11

For in Him we live, and move, and have our being...

Acts 17:28

If You Can Move, You Can Grove

What if we woke up with only the things we thanked God for the day before? My first encounter with this meme really gave me a new perspective on just how grateful I was. Most of us thank God for the home, the car, the job...you know, the bigger things of

The Heart That Smiles

life. But what about those smaller things, like the ability to be able to use all of our senses He blessed us with? In addition to all the material things He's blessed us with, what about thanking Him for the eyes to see all of our blessings, the ears to hear them, and the feet and hands to interact with them? I will elaborate more on the profound blessings of being able to use your senses on Day 17. For now, let us focus on the blessing of mobility.

Most of us go to bed with thoughts of the next day's activities, and most of those activities will involve you being able to move around in order to be productive and progressive. A majority of morning prayers begin with, "Thank you God for another day." How often do we add, "And thank you, God, for my ability to move"? This is something to be overjoyed about. My family and friends that I'm really close to know that I'm a morning person. Yes, I am excited early in the morning…it used to be a general excitement. But now, it's more of an excitement of gratitude. When I wake in the mornings, sure…I thank God for this brand new day I have never seen, but I go on to thank Him for being able to spring out of bed to be productive. Because, if you can move…you can groove.

You can groove to the day's mandatory tasks, extracurricular activities, and not to forget--the day's abundance of opportunities to be progressive. Your being, the maintenance and the continuance of it, are due to the power and providence of God.

DAY 11

Og Mandino reminds us to count our blessings, "Once you realize how valuable you are and how much you have going for you, the smiles will return, the sun will break out, the music will play, and you will finally be able to move forward the life God intended for you with grace, strength, courage, and confidence."

I smiled today because/when...

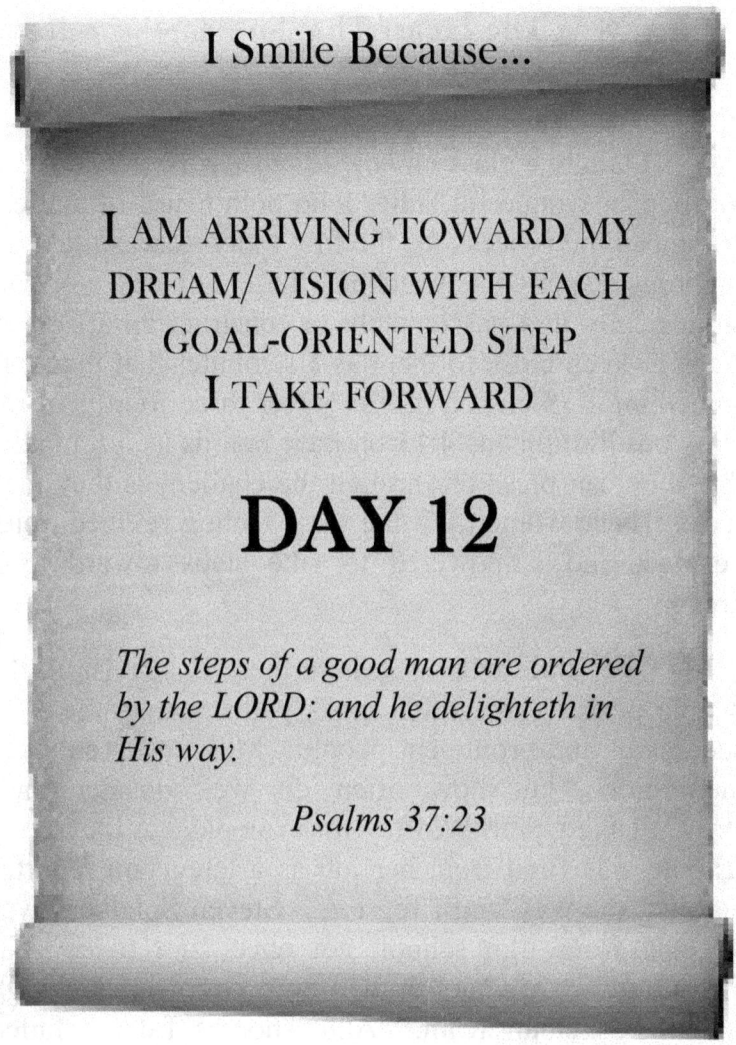

I Smile Because...

I AM ARRIVING TOWARD MY DREAM/ VISION WITH EACH GOAL-ORIENTED STEP I TAKE FORWARD

DAY 12

The steps of a good man are ordered by the LORD: and he delighteth in His way.

Psalms 37:23

Taking Steps Toward the Vision

When we become individuals in whom God delights, we become individuals who follow God, trust God, and carry out God's will for our lives. If you are in need of direction on where to go in life, it is imperative that you seek God first before you take the first step.

The Heart That Smiles

I taught a class on *how to make a vision board* to a group of wonderful ladies who both heard of and experienced the process for the first time. It was the most vigorous experience watching these novices work so strategically and passionately to construct an art of visions to keep close to them as a reminder that they had something to focus on in life. Over three-fourths of the class put Philippians 4:13 on their boards as a reminder that they can press on through the challenges they may face. These women left the class feeling revived, rejuvenated, and empowered to take steps toward their dreams.

The Bible tells us, where there is no vision, the people perish. We often cross paths with some very successful and prominent people. Most of us only see their glory, but how often do we consider their story? Take Oprah Winfrey for example...at the age of 22, she was fired from her job as a television reporter because she was "unfit for TV." Steven Spielberg was rejected from film school, not once...not twice...but three times. Michael Jordan was cut from his high school basketball team. And Thomas Edison failed some 10,000 times before successfully inventing the light bulb. A friend of mine became a well-known speaker after growing up with a speech impediment. What did these successful, talented people have in common? They chose to continue with their visions despite failure and rejection.

DAY 12

Faith is like the propellant to your vision. It is the substance of things hoped for, the evidence of things not seen (Hebrews 11:1). Vision is a mental picture of what's to come...an idea of what the future could hold but has not yet happened. It is the concept inside of us that guides our desire to create. We are all blessed with an amazing gift--the gift of imagination. We have an uncanny ability to take a thought, utilize it, and bring it to life. Vision embodies our hopes and brings us flashes or glimpses of what is possible--so much so, I've heard others say they feel they're so close to their vision that they can just reach out and touch it. With vision, we have a sense of purpose. "Your vision will become clear only when you can look into your own heart. Who looks outside, dreams; who looks inside, awakes." (Carl Jung)

I smiled today because/when...

I Smile Because...

I CHOOSE TO SEE MYSELF THE WAY GOD SEES ME

DAY 13

I will praise thee; for I am fearfully and wonderfully made: marvelous are Thy works; and that my soul knoweth right well.

Psalms 139:14

God Sees You As Royalty

It took me a really long time to accept the way I look. I have one of the most beautiful personalities, but I often asked God why He didn't make all of us pretty. I did not value my unique appearance; instead I despised it. Not only did I not see myself for how other

The Heart That Smiles

people saw me, I also did not see myself for how God saw me.

I was in the eighth grade when my mom asked me if I was going to participate in the school's pageant. I gave her a look as if she had just spoken something foreign to me. She really wanted me to get involved, and she was elated about the fact that she could even make me a dress for the pageant. I remember saying to her, "But I'm not pretty enough." Then the cliches began to rain… "You are beautiful. True beauty is on the inside. You are beautiful inside and out. God made you wonderful, and He looks at you like His princess." I was tuning her out until she said God saw me as a princess. This changed my perception of how I looked. I ended up being in the pageant and won "Miss Congeniality." I no longer despised my appearance. I embraced it and thanked God for making me wonderful and unique.

God sees us as royalty because we are His heirs. God is love, and because of His love and grace, He handpicked us (Ephesians 1:4). Before we were born, before the very foundation of the earth, God knew us, planned for us, and chose us. There are times when we may get overlooked and it causes us to feel worthless or not as good as the next person. It's at these moments that we must remember the truth: We are God's most valued possession…the apple of His eye. He knows everything about us, even the number of hairs on

DAY 13

our heads. He chose us to be holy and set apart, for Himself. So the next time you're feeling a little worthless, please remember that God handpicked you Himself, and you carry a very special treasure on the inside of you that has enormous value, significance, and purpose.

I smiled today because/when...

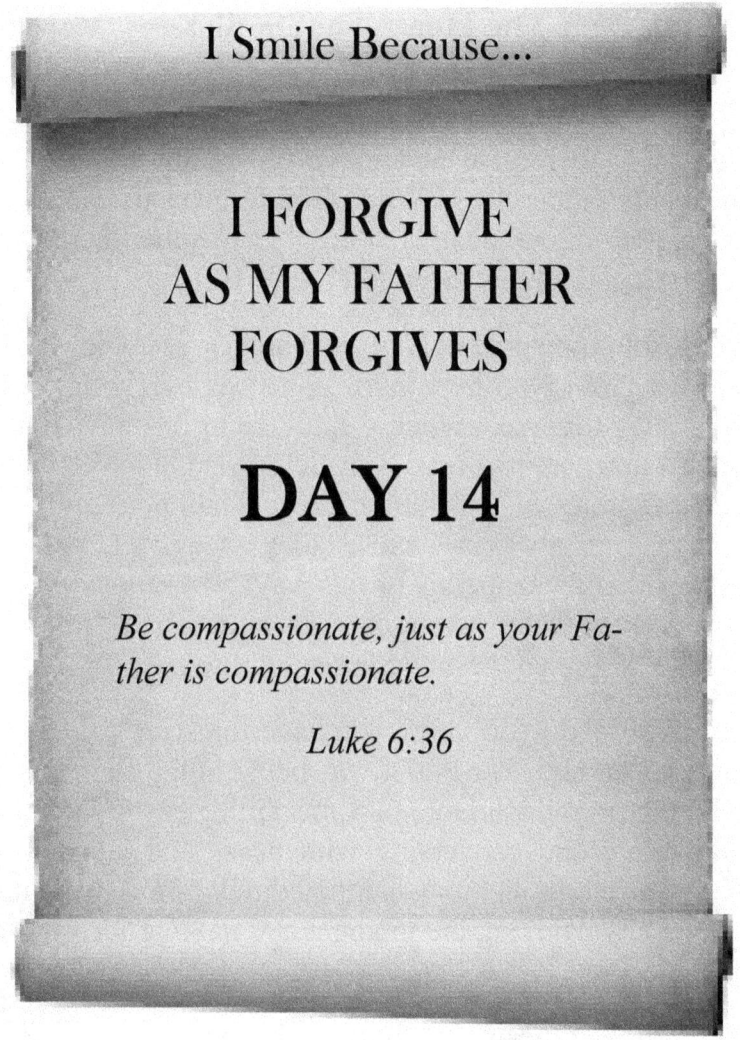

Forgiving as The Father

    Forgiveness is a touchy subject for many of us. We will often say we have forgiven, but still struggle with what was done and how much it hurt. Whether we have been wronged or wronged someone else, it is

The Heart That Smiles

inevitable to forgive and move on. This is what our Heavenly Father does. When God forgives us, He separates us from our sins. He doesn't remember them. He forgives and forgets them. (Hebrews 10:17)

In Romans 12, Paul encourages us to love and forgive those who have hurt us instead of giving them what they deserve. When we adhere to this advice, we open ourselves to break a cycle of retaliation and receive the blessing of mutual reconciliation. Forgiving compassionately may cause the wrongdoer to feel ashamed and change his or her ways. But most importantly, even if the wrongdoer never repents--forgiving them will free you from a burden of bitterness.

How do you know you have forgiven, forgotten, and moved on? For me, it was being in the same room with the person who had hurt me, sitting at the same table, eating and conversing with peace and laughter... never once bringing up what they did or how it made me feel. Only enjoying the moment and looking forward to future ones.

Sometimes we need to forgive ourselves, and this can be harder than forgiving someone else. It is so important that we be honest with ourselves about the good and the bad...pretending that something, never happened or that maybe it will go away...sounds nice but doesn't free us from the bondage it has over us. We are imperfect people which means we are prone to making mistakes in life. We will hurt others sometimes, and we

DAY 14

will have regrets sometimes. We also have the choice to hold on or to let go. And from personal experience, I can assure you that letting go will leave you smiling from the heart.

I smiled today because/when...

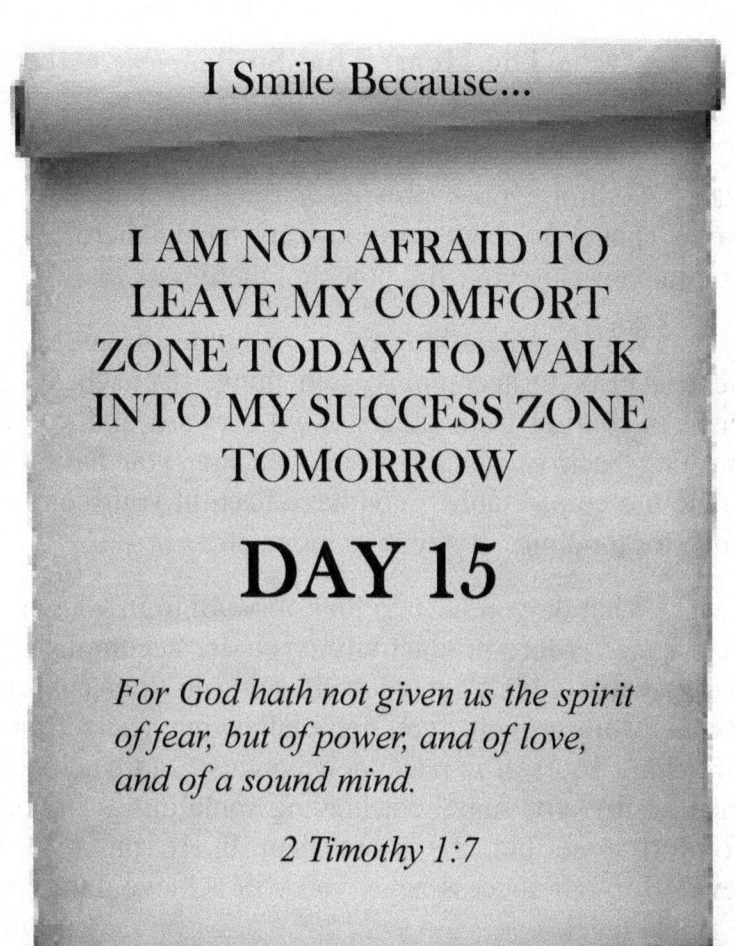

Stepping Into Your Success Zone

    Leaving your comfort zone can be a daunting experience only if you allow it to be. Our comfort zones are those behavioral spaces where our activities and behaviors fit a routine and pattern that minimize stress and

The Heart That Smiles

risk. Comfort zones provide a state of mental security. That's fine, but are you truly happy there? Are you maximizing your full potential there?

We all need a little push sometimes to get to the next level or to accomplish something. But when that push is coming from others to go forward and you're pushing back to remain where you are, you have become too comfortable. You have been in your comfort zone for too long. It's time to move out.

What do you have to look forward to in your success zone? More productivity…you are accomplishing things you couldn't see yourself doing in your comfort zone. More growth…you are challenging yourself and stretching yourself to reach new heights. More achievement…sure, you may be achieving some things in your comfort zone but it's more than likely on a local level. In your success zone, you will achieve things on a global level.

My friend Lenzy was an administrative assistant at a satellite university. A job opening came up for an Admissions Counselor. Lenzy talked about how much she would love to be in this position before it even became available. I just knew she would apply for it and get the job. The office loved her, she was great at what she did, and she was great with the staff and students. Lenzy's problem was giving more respect to her limitations than to her abilities. She didn't think she was qualified enough. Even after the director himself

DAY 15

encouraged her to apply, she refused. She didn't believe she could do the job, and she was too afraid to even try. Unfortunately, the opportunity to be promoted to a higher level position passed Lenzy by. But the story doesn't end there. The position opened again and this time Lenzy stepped into it. Eventually she realized that she had a right to be and walk in all that God had destined for her. When she put her trust in her limits, she stayed comfortable and was viewed as such. When she put her trust in God, she took a step and became successful. Whatever you put your trust in, you give it your power.

I smiled today because/when...

I Smile Because...

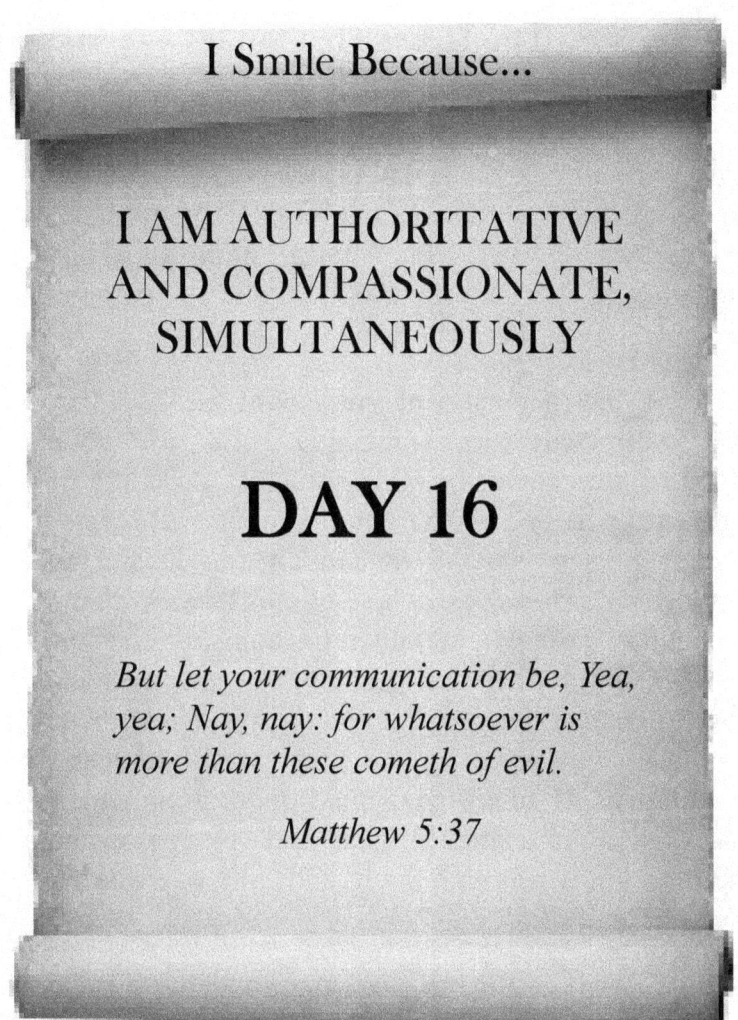

I AM AUTHORITATIVE AND COMPASSIONATE, SIMULTANEOUSLY

DAY 16

But let your communication be, Yea, yea; Nay, nay: for whatsoever is more than these cometh of evil.

Matthew 5:37

Effective Communication

Are you a person of your word, or do you often find yourself coming up with excuses for why you didn't show up to help out with this or that? Many of us even have the urge to say, "I promise" when we commit

The Heart That Smiles

to a project or task. Today's society uses such oaths to back up their words of commitment or cordial statements like, "I'll try," knowing all along they have no intention of carrying them out. Some say patience has become a lost art...I say being truthful has.

Being a person of your word means when you say you will do something, it's as good as done. Emergencies or other situations do come up and prevent us from carrying out a commitment. This is an inconvenience you did not anticipate...This is understandable. However, when circumstances change to something you would rather be doing than what you have committed to, and you don't even have the courtesy to contact the person to whom you made the promise...then you have broken your word and lost some credibility. If this is you most of the time...then you have a serious character issue, and you will eventually become known as unreliable and may even be cut off from a friendship.

We should try to stop compromising our character with empty promises. When you say, "I'll help you out," "I'll do it," "I'll pray for you," or "I'll pick you up," you are communicating those things to someone who believes what you have said. You are also committing your reputation and your character. Kevin Hart says to say it with your chest...I say to say it with your heart. Let there be some conviction and compassion with your words. Jesus said that, "every idle word that

DAY 16

men shall speak, they shall give account thereof in the day of judgment." (Matthew 12:36)

Don't worry... if you're not a person of your word but want to do better...there is hope. Be mindful of those things you make promises for. If you're not sure you can deliver, then don't commit. When you know you can't do it...admit it and just say, "No." If you said you would do it, then do your best to fulfill your offer. If you still fail to deliver...don't lie or make an excuse. Just apologize, do what you can to make up for it and do better the next time. Putting these tips into action will have your heart smiling.

I smiled today because/when...

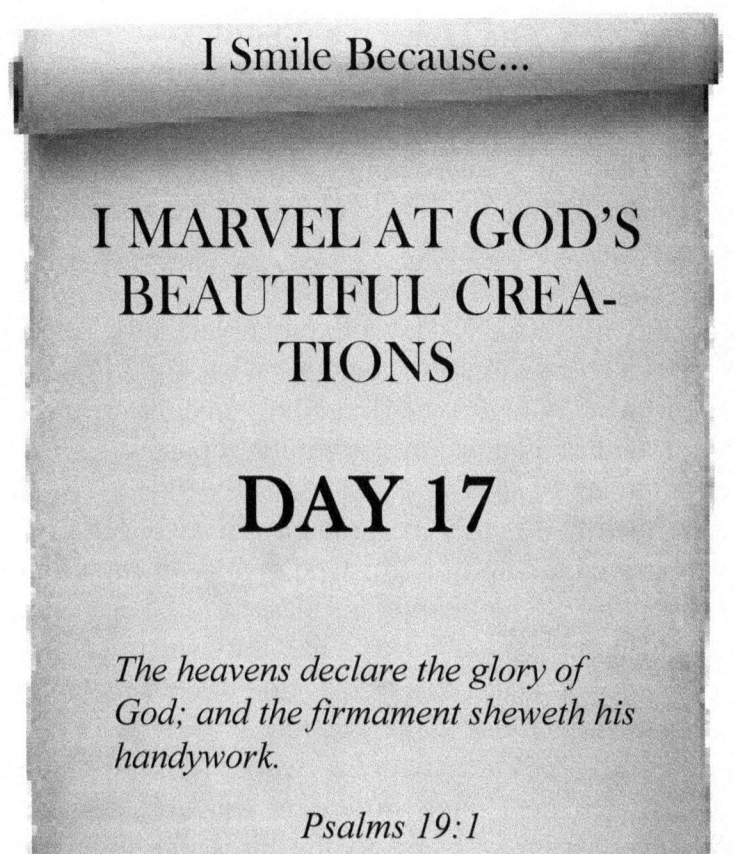

Smell The Roses

    You are probably familiar with the phrase, "Stop and smell the roses." Well, this is more than just a phrase…this is wisdom. God surrounded us with His beautiful creations. He also gave us five senses so that we may fully take pleasure in His works of art. We can

The Heart That Smiles

find God in everything we see, hear, feel, and taste. Using our senses can help us experience His presence all around us.

It is a wonderful feeling to see an image of a dream vacation like Kauai, Hawaii, but to actually set foot there is a more wondrous feeling. What's the first thing you do when you arrive? I can only imagine you looking around in awe as you view this tropical paradise of stunning landscapes and colors. It's like a painting come to life. You were probably in awe before you even arrived taking in all of God's glory in route to the destination. Some people are blessed to have a grand view of mountains and seas; like the owners of homes that are seated near lakes or even the base of mountains, where the hills roll into the sea.

We are blessed with a world full of unique sounds. The next time you are on a nature walk, close your eyes and just listen to the birds chirping, water flowing, the wind blowing, and the stillness. Some of us are even blessed with beautiful melodic voices or the talent to produce harmonious sounds using instruments for others to hear.

Nature also blesses us with a lot of good things to smell and eat. I love to listen to my parents reminisce about their childhood ventures of eating sweetgrass, honeysuckles, polk salad, and bull nettles. I know a thing or two about the sweetgrass and the honeysuckles. A scent or taste has the ability to awaken deep powerful emotions and can often be related to something we connect with like Grandma's biscuits, Mom's

DAY 17

cookies, Dad's sweet potato pie, or even a teacher's scent to create lifelong memories. The next time you eat your favorite citrus fruit, take time to inhale its fragrance, notice it's intricate design of patterns, and then indulge in the burst of its goodness.

Last but certainly not least, we have the sense of touch. Touching provokes a feeling whether it is abstract or textile. This sense of touch also stimulates our emotions and literally touches our hearts. Nature reveals a lot about its Creator—a God of power, intelligence, and intricate detail—a God of order and beauty. It doesn't matter if you're rubbing your fingers on silky rose petals, hugging a loved one, watching a waterfall, listening to your favorite music, or eating your favorite foods, you are bound to smile from your heart.

I smiled today because/when...

I Smile Because...

I ENJOY MAKING SMALL CHANGES THEY LEAD TO A BETTER AND WISER ME

DAY 18

And be not conformed to this world: but be ye transformed by the renewing of your mind, that ye may prove what is that good, and acceptable, and perfect will of God.

Romans 12:2

Building a Stronger You

The key to becoming a powerhouse is to first have your mind set on things that are consistently true and empowering. You can find this in God's word which will never change. Its true purpose remains the

The Heart That Smiles

same--to build you up and give you abundant life. The word does not take anything away from you, but the world will take plenty from you. If you are tired of being in the same unproductive cycle, then a renewing of your mind is inevitable.

When you submit and commit to the transformation, you have an opportunity to rebuild and fill your mind with knowledge and wisdom that will uphold you in the worst of times. Don't expect to become a powerhouse overnight. Transformations require patience and diligence.

Let us compare the renewal of the mind to an old house whose foundation is unstable and rocky and whose frame is shaky. Malachi was a real estate investor who bought old houses to fix up and transform into little castles. They were not like any other houses on the block...they stood out. First, he would examine the house to determine if it needed a few cosmetic repairs or a total gut rehab. He would then put a plan together.

The end result would be a more sturdy, robust, and solid house that someone could now call home.

Now, Let us consider the builder who wants to construct a house to weather the storms. First, he grades and clears the land in preparation for the foundation. Next, he pours the solid foundation on high ground. Then he constructs the framing of the walls and roof. Lastly, he finishes with all of the necessities such as plumbing, electricity, and other necessities.

DAY 18

Rebuilding and renewing your mind is a similar process. In order for renewal to take place, you must remove everything that doesn't belong. You must do a *mind dump* so that you start with a clean, strong, and healthy mental foundation. From there you take it step-by-step and day-by-day, with a new way of thinking. This new way of thinking will help you to develop new habits, which will ultimately give you a new life.

> **"We're controlled by habits,**
> **and our habits are controlled by our thoughts.**
> **Change your mind, change your habits,**
> **and you'll automatically change your life"**
> *Armani Valentino*

Through mind transformation, you can experience the joy you long to bring back into your heart. A transformed mind can help you to be restored, delivered, healed, and elevated!

This is why many Christians believe in a water baptism. Water represents the cleansing and the baptism actually represents the inner renewal or rebirth in the form of a physical act.

The Heart That Smiles

"Why do you want to be baptized? Do you believe that Jesus is the Son of God? Do you believe he died on the cross for the forgiveness of your sins? Do you believe he rose from the dead on the third day and is alive today?"

These were the questions I answered after making the decision to be baptized at 8 years old. The pastor had just finished a sermon about being reborn. He referenced the congregation to Matthew 18:3, "And said, Verily I say unto you, Except ye be converted, and become as little children, ye shall not enter into the kingdom of heaven," and John 3:3, "Jesus answered and said unto him, Verily, verily I say unto thee, Except a man be born again, he cannot see the kingdom of God."

Indeed, I was young but I also had a strong desire to live the way Jesus would have me and to go to heaven. As I got older, I found a need to revisit this strong urgency I had as a child. Did I truly understand what I was committing to at 8 years of age? Did I think it was an automatic ticket to heaven? I'm not sure, but what I am sure of is life for me had become confusing and I was feeling lost in It. The following poem I wrote at age 33 depicts my struggles perfectly:

DAY 18

Who Am I?

The Infamous question, "Who Am I?" Why do I seem to avoid this question each time it arises? Is it simply because I truly don't know, or could it be the question brings about so many disguises?

I've been told I'm too nice, too kind, and oh so sweet...you know—the kind of person most people love to meet. I've also been told I'm really good with math and numbers in particular, but I didn't find a Business Administration major with a minor in Accounting too spectacular. Then I was told by my peers, friends, and especially my mom—You would make a great teacher! Really? Because during my first year of teaching, I was constantly told to get meaner. At this point, I began to feel somewhat like a failure. I couldn't seem to manage my own four children let alone a class of twenty is what I tried to tell her. I even tried nursing...What went wrong there? I really can't say...just decided to go a different way. So, who am I? That is the question. After struggling with this issue for so many years, I finally cried out to God with my face drenched in tears... "What am I supposed to do, Lord? Why am I here? Surely, I have a purpose, but what is it?" Again, who am I—a perception I can't seem to get. Why is it so hard to achieve some resolution to the "Who Am I" pollution? For years, I've allowed others to define me and even control who I am to be. And now, I'm faced with the inevitable: Definition of me by me. So, where do I begin? I'll begin with what

The Heart That Smiles

I know—the facts from the past that no longer show. I know I used to be someone that was driven to succeed and to be the best...someone who would pout if she received less than an "A" on her test. I used to be someone who was always involved in an activity—whether it was a church function, a social club, or just sharing conversation with family. I was smart, full of enthusiasm, and joy. I was free to be me—laugh at anyone... girl or boy. I was often assembled in a place where God should dwell...surrounded by many people who knew Him well. I sought God on a daily basis through prayer and meditation...Always praying for others, from family to those who had received incarceration. I was someone, who at the age of 18, had not found herself nor had any standards that mattered...Someone who entered a committed relationship early and has since lived a life that felt battered. I knew I wanted a man who was smart, fun, who both feared and loved God—and lived by His precepts. I thought I fell in love with this man, but later found, it seemed he only represented the concepts. At the revelation of this acknowledgement, I still decided to stay—thinking that he could change and become my dream husband one day. During the beginning, I did not truly know where to be and who or what to be around. And now, I feel as though I've been really lost...And my request now, more than ever, is to be found. For when rescued by the One God sent as a True Lamb, I then may stand before you and confidently say that which I am! As for now, my search continues to find The Way. However, it feels good to know that I've taken a step in the right direction on this particular day!

DAY 18

What step had I taken? I was tired of being in the same unproductive cycle. A renewing of my mind was inevitable. That day, I surrendered it all to Jesus and allowed Him to occupy all of my heart.

My life did not become a fairytale overnight nor did it become perfect. However, when I turned my life completely over to Jesus, over time, I experienced a transformation that removed a veil from my eyes, my heart, my mind, and my ears that helped me to receive all that God had in store for me. I began living the life I was destined to live. I now love unconditionally and spread the goodness of our Lord and Savior Jesus Christ, every chance I get!

I smiled today because/when...

I Smile Because...

I DON'T GIVE UP BECAUSE OF DESPERATE FEELINGS I'M IN; INSTEAD...
I PUSH ON BECAUSE OF THE DESPERATE FEELINGS THAT ARE IN ME

DAY 19

And let us not be weary in well doing: for in due season, we shall reap, if we faint not.

Galatians 6:9

Desperation Begets Manifestation

Dear Lord,

I pray my son will allow You to guide his future decisions. Bring him peace in areas where he's discouraged and struggling. I pray for his future success in life, that he is able to overcome any challenges that

The Heart That Smiles

crosses his path. Place a confidence in him that he is capable and a strength to keep going. I believe that through You all things are possible! In Jesus' Name, I pray. Amen.

Tension rose in the office as the counselor explained to my son that some of his records were missing and had possibly been lost. According to his transcript, he would have to repeat some classes in order to get the credits he needed to graduate. And if he wanted to graduate on time, he would have to enroll in a self-paced course in addition to his regular classes. My son was already under a lot of stress from being forced to leave his school in Virginia. It was like he lost all motivation and stopped caring. He felt that all the odds were against him. He had made a lot of progress and was excelling in his former school. But due to unforeseen circumstances, he had to leave. It was hurting me to see my baby so discouraged. I did everything I could to remind him of other challenges he'd overcome because he chose to keep going. He wouldn't say anything, but his eyes said to me, "Mom, I don't have any more fight in me. I was working and trying so hard, and look where it got me." He started missing days of school, and his grades began to drop.

While volunteering at a preschool parenting center, I overheard the coordinator say she had received an email from Job Corps by mistake. As I listened to her read the message aloud, I can remember saying, "Thank

DAY 19

You, Jesus! This is exactly what MJ needs!" I asked the coordinator for the contact information and immediately called to set up a meeting with a representative. The following week, the Job Corps representative, two of my son's teachers, his counselor, his principal, myself, and my son all gathered in the conference room to discuss if what Job Corps had to offer would set my son up for future success.

We concluded that it would, and my son left the meeting with a new energy knowing that he had been given an opportunity to get his high school diploma in six months. His new drive and determination helped him to finish the program earlier than expected. And it didn't stop there. He went on to graduate the AR Training Academy as a Corrections Officer for the state of Arkansas where he was the youngest cadet to graduate. And it didn't stop there. In addition to his career, my son became an aspired entrepreneur. He started FlighMo Inc. where the motto is to: **Educate** (Learn Your Dream), **Evaluate** (Test Your Dream), **Edify** (Improve Your Dream), and **Elevate** (Take Flight With Your Dream).

Today when my son encounters other young men who are struggling, he encourages them not to give up. If he could do it, so could they, he says. He goes on to share a quote on one of his t-shirts, "Even if you think you've arrived, never stop "Flighing,"…keep it moving forward and upward!"

The Heart That Smiles

I could not be any more proud of my son, Michael Garland, Jr. (MJ)! He could have left that meeting with the same attitude he had when he entered it. Instead, he chose to fly through the door God opened for him. And today, joy flies within his heart when he smiles.

Because of the desperation that lied within my son to do better and be better, he was able to not only recognize a golden opportunity but to also seize it and use it to his advantage. His company emphasizes being an individual that "flighs" for others too. This is to keep going even if you think you have arrived--you keep moving forward and upward by constantly improving in stature while passing your knowledge or expertise to others...teaching and motivating them to "fligh" for themselves.

I smiled today because/when...

I smiled today because/when...

I Smile Because...

I CHOOSE NOT TO LOSE MYSELF IN OTHERS' MESSES; BUT INSTEAD, BE A LEADER THAT GUIDES THEM TOWARD PEACE AND ORDER.

DAY 20

Let all things be done decently and in order.

1 Corinthians 14:40

From Gossiper to Philosopher

Our God is a God of order and has been since the beginning of time. Without Him, there is nothing but chaos. With diligent and consistent effort, we can keep our living spaces in order, and keeping God at the forefront allows Him to keep our lives in order in every aspect of life.

The Heart That Smiles

In most workplaces, you have coworkers who constantly talk about others and situations that often lead to rumors and leaks of personal or confidential information. This type of gossip causes great distraction and may even wreck careers and reputations. It can be tempting to vent at the office where you spend countless hours with employees that have become your friends or associates outside of work. However, if there is something very personal that you really need to talk about but really need to remain confidential, then find that associate you notice that shuts gossip down when confronted with it; that person who will listen and give sound advice if pulled aside for a private talk. That go-to person was Cianna.

Cianna knew how to be professional and was laid-back at the workplace. However, coworkers knew not to come to her with mess. Cianna was very cautious of who she trusted. She understood that if someone will discuss others with you, they will certainly discuss you with others. However, she was approachable, and some coworkers knew that if they went to her with a personal issue, they wouldn't have to worry about being the topic of gossip central the next day. They could always count on her to provide sound advice and help come up with solutions to bring peaceful and orderly resolutions.

Sure, gossip is common. People like to get a tidbit of "insider knowledge" about others. What is your motive for gossiping or hanging around gossipers?

DAY 20

Is it to discuss others or a situation to get help for the person? Or do you regularly engage in communication that destructively harms others so that you can have something or someone to talk about?

The Bible does address gossip. God tells us that we should not go about as talebearers among our people, spreading slander, and endangering our neighbor's life. (Leviticus 19:16) Instead, we should go about as truth bearers to conceal the matters of the heart of others with encouragement and love.

I smiled today because/when...

I Smile Because...

I CHOOSE TO REPRESENT MY TRUE CHARACTER TO IMPRESS ME AND NOT A PRETENSE CHARACTER TO IMPRESS SOMEONE ELSE

DAY 21

For do I now persuade men, or God? Or do I seek to please men? For if I yet pleased men, I should not be the servant of Christ.

Galatians 1:10

I Am Who I Show I Am?

"When someone shows you who they are, believe them the first time." (Maya Angelou) What a man does has greater influence than what he says. Some people put on acts for approval, to be accepted, or to get whatever they're after.

The Heart That Smiles

Candace and Kyle started dating after crossing paths after 17 years. Kyle had been divorced for 2 years, had 1 child, and was a successful real estate agent. Candace had been divorced for 4 years, had 2 children, and was a struggling career mom. To Kyle, she was a laid-back single mom and successful career woman who was spiritual, secure, and well-composed because that is what she led him to believe. Why wasn't Candace honest about who she really was? Even though she was so broken on the inside, she thought she was ready to be married again. Candace looked at Kyle as a savior…if I can just get this man to commit to me, then everything will be perfect…my kids will have a step-dad, I will have a husband to love me and help me with my bills. After sizing Kyle up, she did everything she could to win him over. She did not want to let this fine, intelligent, successful, God-fearing man pass her by.

What Candace did not realize is that Kyle had already arrived where she needed to go. While she was busy pretending to be his dream woman, she was losing a lot of ground on becoming the woman she needed to be. Her focus was solely on winning his heart, even after she had it. Her facade did not last for long. After holding it together for a couple of months, her truth was revealed.

Kyle was unreachable for hours due to a family emergency involving his grandmother. Candace had prepared dinner at her house and was expecting Kyle to

DAY 21

meet her. At 30 minutes past his time of arrival, she called to see if everything was okay; 45 minutes passed and she left a message to see if he had forgot; an hour passed and she left a message asking if he was still coming. After approximately two hours had passed, she began blowing up his phone and leaving profane messages of accusations, via text and voice mail, that he must be with someone else. And he was, but not in the way she was thinking. He was with his family for support...he did not know if his grandmother would pull through the massive heart attack she had suffered.

The day was almost over, when the thought to call Candace to apologize for not contacting her earlier, crossed his mind. He went to his car, put his phone on the charger, turned it on, and heard alert, after alert, after alert of incoming messages...15 texts and 27 missed calls...all from Candace. The first text read, "Are you okay?" and the text directly below that read, "I hope you're enjoying being with that witch!" And the messages only got worse from there. Kyle did not know what to make of all this...he did a triple take at the phone to make sure those messages were indeed from Candace, and after verifying that they indeed were, he prayed about how to handle the situation and what to say to her.

Kyle too, was longing to have someone in his life...a woman who was smart, fun, successful...who both feared and loved God and lived by His precepts. After witnessing Candace's episode, he felt hurt and now looked at her as someone who only represented those concepts. All he could think about was how good he had been to this woman, and the one time something doesn't go her way, she becomes someone totally different...she becomes her true self. After he had prayed about how to approach Candace and what to say, he called her.

She answered before the first ring ended with an abrupt, "Hello."

In a calm, respectful, yet firm tone, he responded, "Hi Candace. Before you say anything, please allow me to finish what I have to say. My grandmother had a massive heart attack earlier today. I have been with my family all day praying. My mom wants to stay at the hospital, and I am going to stay with her. I apologize for not contacting you earlier. My phone was dead until a few minutes ago. I am going to hang up my phone now. I ask that you not contact me until after you have sought God to give you what you need, because I can't give it to you. I wish you and your children the best. Goodnight." And he hung up.

Candace had a rude awakening. She was seeking Kyle's approval with the wrong motives. Kyle helped her see there was nothing he could do to fix her internally, and that she should be seeking God's approval to become the woman He would have her to be.

I smiled today because/when...

I smiled today because/when...

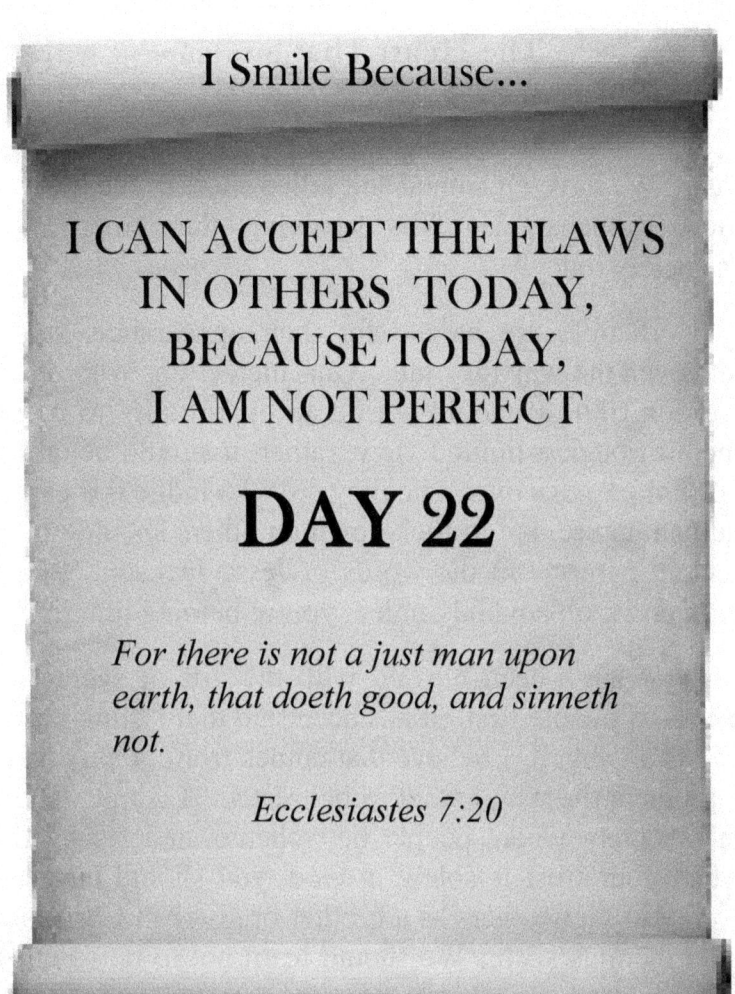

I Smile Because...

I CAN ACCEPT THE FLAWS IN OTHERS TODAY, BECAUSE TODAY, I AM NOT PERFECT

DAY 22

For there is not a just man upon earth, that doeth good, and sinneth not.

Ecclesiastes 7:20

Flaws Exist In All

    The only man to walk this earth who was perfectly just was Jesus Christ himself. While here on earth, Jesus went about doing good and never sinned in all of his life. This cannot be said about any other man. We have all sinned and fallen short of the glory of God. (Romans 3:23) Why is judging others so prevalent in society today?

People are judged for their appearance, status, and even the way they talk. Our interactions with others we don't know should not be an opportunity to define them through a limited view; rather, it should be an opportunity to discover who they are. To judge is a part of human nature, but to look down on others should not be second nature. In the words of Jesse Jackson, "Never look down on anybody unless you're helping him up."

I have been blessed with the gift of seeing the hearts of people first. It has been said that I think everyone is an angel. I believe that comes from merely treating others the way I want to be treated. I admit we live in a society where people lie, scheme, and steal. But when your trust is solely in God, you should have the ability to view others as a brother or sister in Christ and treat them as such. We should learn not to be so quick to see or find something wrong in the next person.

All my life, I have encountered diversity, and I am not only referring to being around others who have a different color of skin than mine. I am also referring to people who have different backgrounds, life experiences, and environments than mine. I have always looked at diversity as a means to share and compare. We can learn so much from each other if we would just give the next person an opportunity to tell

DAY 22

their story; we must listen to them with our hearts, and then help them any way we can.

As a teacher, I found myself giving hugs several times a day to several different students. Each one looked different and came from an array of environments, from stable to not so stable, and well-off to not so well-off. My greetings and hugs were the same for every student...full of love and compassion. I was also faced with several opportunities to improve the life of someone struggling. I tried to take advantage of every chance, because it made me happy to make a difference that caused others to smile from their hearts. Seeing others happy puts joy in my heart. Knowing I helped bring them happiness blesses me with a heart that smiles.

I smiled today because/when...

I Smile Because...

I CHOOSE TO PRAISE GOD DURING HAPPY MOMENTS AND DIFFICULT MOMENTS AND GIVE HIM THANKS FOR EVERY MOMENT

DAY 23

In everything give thanks: for this is the will of God in Christ Jesus.

1 Thessalonians 5:18

Praise the Creator

Do you ever catch yourself being overly grateful when circumstances are in your favor, but when they are overwhelming, you can't seem to find a reason to be so grateful? We should do our best not to let our joy, prayers, and thankfulness fluctuate with our circumstances or feelings.

The Heart That Smiles

Some people misunderstand Paul when he urges us to give thanks for everything. He was not referring to everything that happens to us. Remember, evil does not come from God and the evil acts done against us are not from Him, so we should not thank Him for them. Instead, when harmful circumstances come to overtake us, we can still be thankful for God's presence and His love to get us through these perilous times. We should be thanking God for never leaving us nor forsaking us. He is a just God.

The Mishelin's lost their only son in Iraq, not to the war, but to intentional friendly fire. A comrade of their son had a mental breakdown and began shooting at his fellow soldiers. This horrendous act took the life of a young man who was devoted to his family, and it left his family filled with bitterness and unrelenting pain.

The Mishelin's were a loving family who loved God and were a blessing to many. And although they were grateful for all God had blessed them with, their anguish had them questioning God. They could not understand why He allowed this to happen to their only son. Through all the anguish and pain, it's imperative that we remember God loves us, and He is not the author of tragedy or evil! We live in an imperfect world… a world where people have free-will to love or not to love. It rains on the just and the unjust. Our comfort and peace should lie in the truth of knowing that when tragedy hits home, God is still with us, and He will

DAY 23

cause good to emerge if we're committed to following Him. In their son's honor, the Mishelin's started a foundation that supports families of those suffering from PTSD as well as families grieving from losing a loved one. They are allowing God to use them to raise awareness and to help bring healing to broken families in hopes that joy will reign once again in their hearts.

I smiled today because/when...

I Smile Because...

SOMEONE REFUSES TO GIVE ME CLOSURE, AND I SEARCH DEEP WITHIN TO LET IT GO AND GET MY OWN HAPPY ENDING

DAY 24

Peace I leave with you, my peace I give unto you: not as the world giveth, give I unto you. Let not your heart be troubled, neither let it be afraid.

John 14:27

Don't Lose Composure Over No Closure

Jesus lets us know that the end result of the Holy Spirit's work in our lives is deep and lasting peace. In the world, we will experience a lot of conflict. But Jesus says that if we are willing to accept, He will give us a peace that is confident assurance in any circumstance.

The Heart That Smiles

It doesn't matter if you were let go in a marriage, from a sport's team, or on a job without any explanation, Jesus has promised you the inheritance of peace. You can prevail.

Erin was devastated when she was called into her boss's office and unexpectedly told that her position was no longer needed and that her office should be cleared out by the following day. A million thoughts raced through Erin's mind with the first being, "But why...what did I do?" After giving this company her blood, sweat, and tears, she was let go for no valid reason. She felt betrayed.

This job was all Erin knew and her only source of income. As she was packing up her office, the walk into her boss's office to receive that unimaginable news played over and over again in her mind. She wanted to scream and destroy some things. All she had were visions of her losing her assets and never finding another job. All that she was and had accomplished, while working for this company took a backseat while she grieved over her loss for several weeks.

Erin was, what most would call, a lukewarm Christian...she occasionally attended church. While in between jobs, Erin had more time on her hands than she knew what to do with. She saw herself heading toward depression, and wanted to nip it in the bud before it became a reality. She started to take advantage of her extra time by spending it studying the Bible. She went to

DAY 24

church a lot more and even became more involved. She was beginning to thrive with an inner peace knowing that all was well.

Erin began to discover that she was so much more than that job. She spent several nights crying like a baby because there was never any valid closure to why her firm let her go. Erin finally accepted that closure may never come and that it was time for her to find her own...she instinctively knew that she would never work for anyone again. She made some sacrifices by moving out of her beautiful condo and moving in with her mom, cutting her personal expenses almost to the bare bone, and using her savings to invest in some photography equipment.

After finding her own closure, Erin picked up an old hobby and passion of photography, spent more time with family, volunteered at local schools and shelters. Eventually her hobby turned into a successful business, and she was able to continue doing all of her extras while doing what she loved...blessing others with lasting impressions of smiles from their hearts.

The Individuals of Extraordinary Faith place an Impression on the Heart of God when they take a leap into the unknown, not worrying about what others are doing or thinking; instead, they delight themselves in the Lord and place their trust solely in Him. They are not easily offended when the outcome doesn't come when and how they want it--They keep asking, seeking,

The Heart That Smiles

and knocking in pursuit of God's Favor--They keep believing for their Extraordinary Faith to bring them to an Extraordinary Expected End! They cause the Heart of God to Smile!

I smiled today because/when...

I smiled today because/when...

I Smile Because...

I GET A CLEAR UNDERSTANDING INSTEAD OF MAKING REGRETFUL ASSUMPTIONS

DAY 25

Wisdom is the principal thing; therefore get wisdom: and with all thy getting get understanding.

Proverbs 4:7

Having Whole Wisdom

The Book of Proverbs is full of lessons on how to attain wisdom, discipline, and a prudent life…how to do what is right, just, and fair. Solomon urges us to go after God's wisdom and to seek it on a daily basis. Accepting the word of God and learning His com-

The Heart That Smiles

mands are prerequisites for becoming wise. His word tells us to develop an "ear" for understanding and set our hearts to receive it. We must also be willing to call and cry out for wisdom, and pursue it like a great treasure (Proverbs 1-4).

It is possible for a person to have wisdom but no understanding of the knowledge. Understanding is the ability to perceive and discern a situation in order to apply wisdom. However, when we understand how to apply the knowledge God has given us, we are operating in, what I call, "whole wisdom."

I have had the privilege of meeting some very intellectual and interesting people over the years, some of which were through my former employment, and others through conferences, retreats, and other social gatherings. Some of these people made a huge impact on my life, my views, and my personal philosophy. One such person would be my very own Auntie Selma.

Auntie Selma is our family's matriarch. She is the "Proverbs 31" woman, and she is rare. My auntie lives her life with discretion and prudence. Her discretion has preserved her and me at times. Her discernment has always been on point concerning some of my life's encounters. There is no wonder her favorite animal is the elephant--she too, is full of grace and wisdom. She fears the Lord and values her relationship with Him. This is wise, and wise is she.

DAY 25

Through God's Holy Spirit, wisdom can empower you to make good, righteous choices that will lead to a heart that smiles!

I smiled today because/when...

I Smile Because...

I PUT ASIDE
MY PRIDE
AND ALLOW OTHERS
TO HELP ME

DAY 26

Pride goeth before destruction; and a haughty spirit before a fall.

Proverbs 16:18

Pride Won't Be My Downside

Although pride has been defined as a feeling of deep pleasure or satisfaction in an achievement, accomplishment, or in someone or something else, it is most commonly thought of as conceit, egotism, stubbornness, vanity, or vainglory, all over one's own appearance or status in life.

The Heart That Smiles

Proud people tend to self-attribute a sense of worth that is easily overvalued, overinflated, and maybe even unrealistic. It's ironic that most proud people who carry this inwardly directed emotion, called pride, don't even realize it as their problem. Pride can be destructive. It will keep a person from apologizing even when they know they are wrong. It will even keep you cornered in a room of familiarity instead of venturing out to try new things...you don't want to look like you may feel--inadequate. Pride will cause you to act out of character to simply make a meaningless point.

Even shyness is a form of pride. Joyce Meyer brought this type of self-consciousness into perspective when she said, "When you're so consumed with what people think of you, how they will treat you, and what you're going to do when the spotlight is on you, you're self-centered. You are the center of your thought life. It's the last place you need to be."

Joah didn't realize he was full of pride, but everyone else around the office did. Did he say he was a team-player on his application? If he did--that was a bold face lie. He never allowed anyone to help him whether it was through constructive criticism or just lending a helping hand. Joah carried himself as if he was Superman. He wore invisible capes and name tags that read, "Hello: My name is Joah. I know everything. I can save myself. I can heal myself. And I can keep myself from harm." So, if he had such a handle on

DAY 26

his job, why was his self-appraisal form turned in incorrect and incomplete? It was given back to him to correct and complete...which one of us will he ask for help? If Joah was stubborn like this on the job, he was probably just as or even more prideful with other aspects of his life.

The Bible tells us that the arrogance of man will be brought low and the pride of men humbled (Isaiah 2:17). Pride has to go for there to be room for God to reign as Lord in our hearts.

I smiled today because/when...

I Smile Because...

I CHOOSE TO STAY CLEAR OF TEMPTATION THAT WILL BRING HARM TO MYSELF OR TO OTHERS

DAY 27

There hath no temptation taken you but such as is common to man: but God is faithful, who will not suffer you to be tempted above that ye are able; but will with the temptation also make a way to escape, that ye may be able to bear it.

1 Corinthians 10:13

Lead Us Not Into Temptation

I have this friend…we'll call her, Wen. Wen is one of the most beautiful and sweet-hearted persons you may ever meet. However, Wen can have a short temper and one of her favorite phrases is, "Girl, please pray for me because I'm about to catch a case." And what do I

The Heart That Smiles

do? I pray. Because I know she's not playing. You do not want to get on her bad side.

The good news is, temptations happen to everyone, and many have resisted them. Yes, God gives us a way of escape. One step to resisting temptation, is to recognize those people and situations that make you want to "catch a case" or just give you trouble in general. Run from people and situations you know are wrong...trouble is written all over them with flashing bright neon colors...again, I say, Run! It may not be easy, but try and choose to do what is right. Pray about it, like Kyle from Day 21...I know that brother wanted to go off, but he chose to stay calm, and he ran. He probably should have told her to lose his number, but he was like, call me after you have had a meeting with Jesus!

Like Wen, seeking friends who love God and can offer help when you are tempted, will provide you an intercession to go in a different direction. Wen's career brings her in contact with several people each day. These people are often rude and a challenge to deal with. So, by now, you know I like to use poetic catchy little phrases to help put me in calm mode. I shared these with Wen to use when she finds herself about to go there: "Rude Dude, Go Away and Come Back Some Other Day...When I'm Not Here" or "Drama Mama, Go Away and Come Back Some Other Day...When I'm Not Here" and my favorite, "Stay Calm and Recite a

DAY 27

Psalm"--(then start saying your favorite Psalm). I encouraged Wen to use the latter phrase because I'm afraid she may slip up one day and say the first two out loud to the customer.

God is faithful. He does not allow any temptation to come our way that is too great for us to resist. He always provides a way for us to say no and the strength to run. We should always remember that there is no temptation that comes our way that is beyond the course of what others have had to face, including Jesus Himself. Thus comes the phrase, "What would Jesus do?" It wouldn't hurt to ask yourself this the next time you are faced with temptation.

I smiled today because/when...

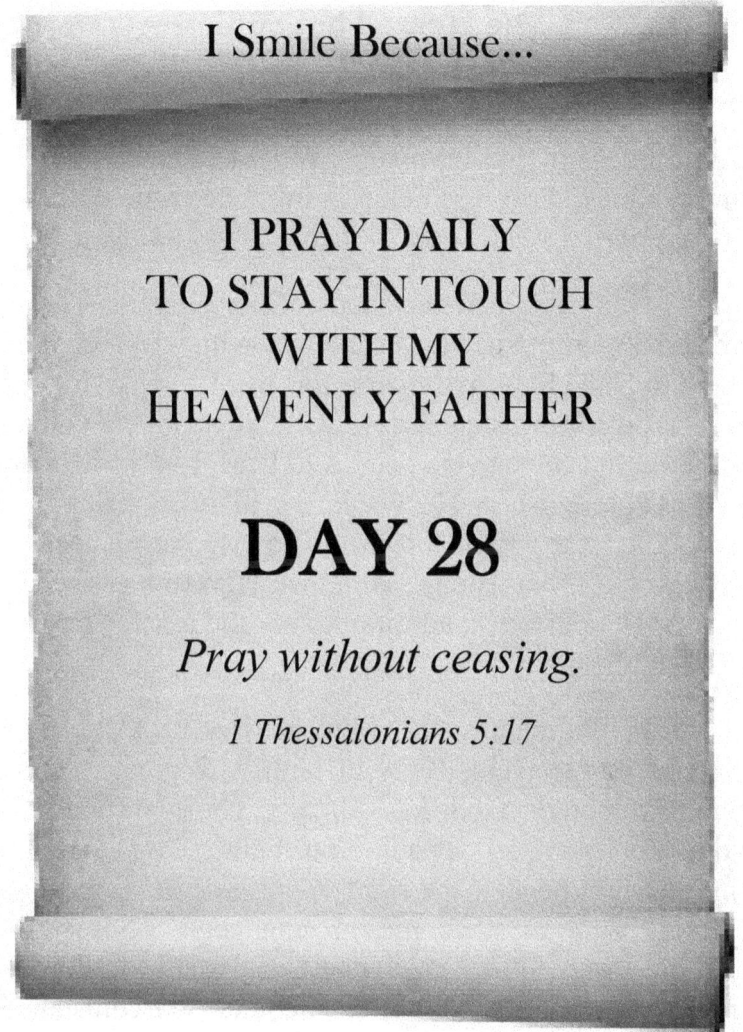

Pray About Everything Everyday

    We may pray in different ways at different stages of our lives. And sometimes, our way of praying changes as we grow in our connection to God. Prayer is a relationship, wherein we humbly communicate. We share or exchange information, news, or ideas. We interact, converse, commune. We talk together with pro-

The Heart That Smiles

found intensity and intimacy. We interchange thoughts and feelings. Prayer is being in intimate communication and rapport.

God should be the focus of our prayers. He is a personal being that we can interact with. He is always there to listen to us and to comfort us. He looks forward to hearing from us each day. God is omnibenevolent-- all loving. I believe He desires to hear from us as much as possible because He wants a real relationship with us. When we go to God in prayer, we can thank Him for His gifts to us, praise Him, ask Him to bless others, ask for His guidance, admit our sins and ask for forgiveness and help.

In Philippians 4:2, Paul advises us to turn our worries into prayers. Pray in faith with great expectation...as though God has already come through for you. For example, "Thank You, Father God, for sending the right people, the right opportunity, and the right breaks for me to overcome this challenge." Sometimes this may seem like a challenge because life on the job, in the home, or at school often encounters circumstances that cause us to get anxious or to worry. Whenever you start to worry, stop and pray. Tell God what you need and thank Him for all He has done, is doing, and will do.

I used to be a big worrier. I stressed and fretted over so many things—even things that were beyond my control. The way I prayed showed it. I can only imag-

DAY 28

ine that God was saying, "My daughter is so dramatic. She comes to me as though she doesn't trust that I have all power and total control." The truth is I didn't. My trust was not solely in God. I couldn't see beyond the now, and I prayed as if my world was coming to an end instead of God bringing an end to my worries by praying for peace. Today, I am a Prayer Warrior instead of a Prayer Worrier.

I am so glad I retrained my mind, which had a transforming effect on how I prayed. Now when I pray, I give God my worry and thank Him in advance for covering, delivering, and restoring, even though they haven't manifested in my life yet. But praying in this way gives me the faith that they will. This is how our Savior, Jesus Christ, prayed--what could be more powerful than that! Always remember that no matter where you are or what you're doing, you can approach God in prayer about anything, for He will always be there to listen to you…to listen to your heart. And don't forget to cast all your worries upon Him so that you can feel joy and smile from the heart everyday!

I smiled today because/when...

I Smile Because...

I AM ORGANIZED AND PREPARED TO IMPLEMENT OPPORTUNITIES OF SUCCESS FOR MYSELF AND OTHERS

DAY 29

The ants are a people not strong, yet they prepare their meat in the summer.

Proverbs 30:25

Plan. Prepare. Produce.

Many of us are familiar with Aesop's Fable, <u>The Ant and The Grasshopper</u>, probably from childhood. However, this fable isn't just for kids any more... some of us adults can learn a lot from this story too. If you've never read the story, I can sum it up quickly by

The Heart That Smiles

saying the grasshopper decided to play all summer long while the ant used his time wisely and gathered food to store for winter. Once winter set in, the ant had plenty to eat while the foolish grasshopper starved. Like me, the grasshopper learned that procrastination can lead to an unwanted destination.

How you live your life today is preparing you for tomorrow…for success or failure. My daughter wanted to learn how to play her clarinet better. There were several free videos on YouTube with clarinet lessons for the beginner: teaching yourself to play. I helped Nyah bookmark a few of them. I expected her to come home with her clarinet each day to practice, but she would only bring it home a couple of times during the week. And on the days she did have it, her tablet was consumed with social media screens instead of the videos that would teach her to play the clarinet. She did not plan to prepare for improvement in playing the clarinet, so when it came to her first concert…she begged not to participate because she couldn't produce like she wanted.

On another occasion, my middle son wanted to learn how to drive. We went by the local police headquarters to pick up a driver's manual. When we returned home, he placed the manual on his desk. Besides flipping through it on the way home, he never opened it to study over a matter of weeks. The manual was just sitting on his desk waiting for him to open it. He would

DAY 28

get ready for school, go to school, come home, eat supper, play Xbox, watch television, and play a little more Xbox before it was time to go to bed and start all over again the next day. Yet, he wanted to take my car for a drive. I don't think so, Buddy…he had done absolutely nothing to prepare for getting behind the wheel of my car. John Maxwell reminds us that, "You will never change your life until you change something you do daily."

I smiled today because/when...

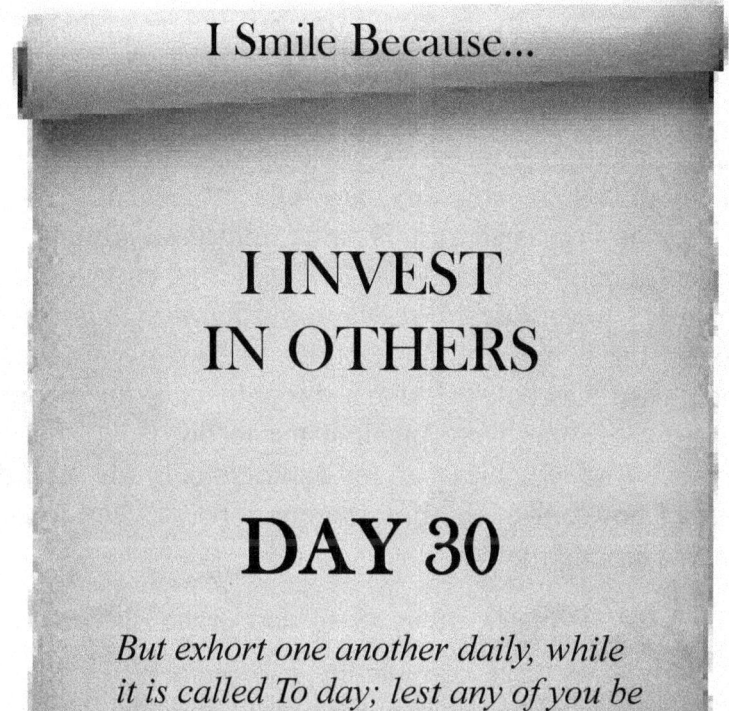

I Smile Because...

I INVEST IN OTHERS

DAY 30

But exhort one another daily, while it is called To day; lest any of you be hardened through the deceitfulness of sin.

Hebrews 3:13

Investing in Others

    I have a deep compassion for the Lord...a deep compassion for people...and a deep compassion to see others happy and fulfilled...to see others Smile...From the Heart! During the journey of finding myself and discovering who God designed me to be, I came to

The Heart That Smiles

realize that my ministry is not only one of Godly love but compassion, empathy, and encouragement. I believe many of us share this same ministry. Although I haven't completely arrived to the expected end God has for me, I have a desire to share my journey thus far in hopes that it may motivate others to take steps toward their own success. God has brought amazing people into my life that have inspired me to do better and be better…And to achieve all my aspirations in life regardless of how out of the box they may be. I want to see people around me win!

The Bible heartens us to encourage one another on a daily basis, as often as there is an occasion and an opportunity for it. Time is precious, and we should use it while we have it. A former pastor once said, "What you make happen for others, God will make happen for you." While financial investing can deem risky, investing in the lives of others for the Glory of Christ will always provide a positive return.

As a mother and teacher, I am flooded with opportunities to invest in my children, students, parents, and coworkers. My son, Trey, is extremely gifted in art and has been since he was about six years old. In addition to constant words of encouragement, his dad and I have given him countless sketch pads and art kits for him to grow his talent.

Teachers work extremely hard before school even starts to establish a safe and welcoming classroom

DAY 30

environment. During the first few weeks of school, they work even harder to get to know their students and build rapport with them. Investing emotionally in my students and building positive relationships with their parents, inspired them to be passionate in their learning at school and at home. As you've probably guessed, I invested in my coworkers with a smile each and every day, several times a day…thus came my nickname, Smiley, thanks to Mrs. Kayla-Mayla Bowden.

Our wonderful God created everyone with unique abilities and talents to help serve each other. Sometimes, one may not recognize things or need guidance in developing it through others' time, knowledge, and resources. We should start investing in the youth of today at a young age. Let us help them to recognize their strengths and then develop them. Their hearts will remain full of joy that we did!

I smiled today because/when...

I Smile Because...

I LOVE MYSELF BY NOURISHING MY MIND, BODY, AND SOUL WITH POSITIVE THOUGHTS, NUTRITIOUS FOODS, AND GOD'S WORD

DAY 31

For no man ever yet hated his own flesh, but nourisheth and cherisheth it, even as the Lord the church.

Ephesians 5:29

Loving Yourself Completely

It took me years to grasp the concept that my body is not my own, and is the temple of the Holy Spirit. There are many people who think they have a right to do whatever they want with their own bodies. The flesh is weak indeed, and we often give in to its

The Heart That Smiles

cravings—what it lusts for. No matter how much we desire to be free with our bodies, it actually does matter what we do with them. God's Word specifically tells us to honor Him with our bodies. There is a binding relationship between the physical and the spiritual.

Sexual immorality and over indulgence in the wrong foods are not the only things that defile the body. Every part of your body is an instrument. We can defile the body with our eyes by what we watch on television, social media, the music we listen to, or the words we read in books.

With our ears, by what we listen to. With our mouths, by what we speak. With our hands, by what and how we give. With our feet, by where we allow them to take us.

Dr. Randy's affirmation, "I love myself by nourishing my mind, body, and soul," became one of my favorites to cite. When I finally comprehended that honoring God with my body was to present it as a living sacrifice, holy and acceptable to Him for His glorification, I gained a greater appreciation of the gift I had been loaned. (Romans 12:1) This both convicted me and inspired me to retrain my mind. I began nourishing my mind, body, and soul with positive thoughts, nutritious food, and the Word of God.

Each morning, I wake up expressing love to God in prayer of how thankful I am to be able to see a new

DAY 31

day. Then, I express love to myself by giving me a big squeezable hug and saying, "I love you because you are a radiant masterpiece wonderfully made by the Creator Himself, whose Spirit dwells on the inside of you… to guide you… in all you set out to do!" These regimens are part of my morning routine, which is critical to having some consistency in your life. Other morning habits include meditation, a quick workout, and then my favorite breakfast of coconut pancakes and green milk (almond and coconut milk blended with kale, spinach, and banana). I hardly ever run out of pancake mix, but if I lack any ingredients for green milk (other than milk), I would fix a green tea and coconut latte. After I've nourished my mind, body, and soul, I wake my kiddos and love on them.

Loving yourself completely is the prerequisite to loving others unconditionally and living a joyful life. It is a process, but when you start to love yourself more each day, it's amazing how your life will improve. You start to feel better, you're more productive, your relationships with others become better, and…you start to smile a lot more from the heart!

Note from Author:

If we ever cross paths,
I want to see you "Smiling Too For You!"

I smiled today because/when...

I smiled today because/when...

Acknowledgements

To My Heavenly Father: *You constantly make me smile. I acknowledge You with the utmost admiration, appreciation, and love. Thank You for placing this project in my spirit to share with the world. I give You the Glory and the Honor!*

To My Mother, Lucinda Gordon: *Your unconditional love and guidance has helped me to soar. You are the wind beneath my wings. I thank you for never giving up on me and for always pushing me to keep going on my journey despite the many roadblocks I encountered. Thanks for always interceding for me through prayer. You have always supported my ventures no matter how out of the box they have been. My heart smiles because of your love, your grace, and your endless support!*

To My Father (Roosevelt Furlow Jr.) and My Brother (Shun Furlow): *Thank you for always encouraging me, praying for me, and believing in my every endeavor!*

To My Children (Michael, Trevion, Nyah, and Christian Garland): *You are my heartbeats and my motivation. Thank you for never doubting that I would pull through and leave you a legacy. You make my heart leap with joy!*

To My Mentors (Aunt Ann Gordon, Aunt Selma Benjamin, Aunt Glory Hardy, Aunt May Foreman, Aunt Pat Washington, Dr. Michele R. Wright, and Tiffany W. Washington): *Thank you for your endless support and love!*

Acknowledgements

To My Spiritual Moms (Becky Christian and Betty Walton): *You are my angels. Thank you for your constant reminder to keep Jehovah God at the forefront of all I set out to do!*

To My Pastors (Apostle Charles and Neatrice Gordon, Kenneth and First Lady Debra Anderson, Donald and Lady Wendy Vaughn, Don and First Lady Lynn White): *Thank you for being part of the village that raised me and guided me to be the woman I am today!*

To My Best Friends (LaShunda Cox, Portia Washington, and Tasha Mahomes): *Thank you beautiful ladies for always keeping it positive!*

To My Angels Who Are No Longer With Me (Grandmother Catherine Furlow, Grandmother Mary Gordon, and Auntie Linda Stephens): *You always inspired my heart to smile through your constant spirits of joy!*

To My Publisher, Armani Valentino: *Your drive, wisdom, and intelligent guidance continue to bring the best out of me!*

To My Bestie, Ladera "Dee" Northcross: *Thanks for being my friend and my lifeline. You have always pushed me to embrace who I am, march to the beat of my own drum, and to always stay true to myself. You have been like a big sister to me, and I am forever grateful for your love and support.*

To My Best Friend Guy, (You Know Who You Are): *Thank you for being the reason my heart smiles no matter what kind of mood I'm in.*

AUTHOR'S BIO

Born Shelda Evette Furlow, Shelda Evette is an aspiring writer, compassionate teacher, and source of inspiration within her community. Shelda grew up in the small city of Camden, Arkansas where she was close to family and active in her church. She married young and became the mother of four beautiful angels.

Shelda has never lost her love and deep compassion for God and people. She loves helping and serving others. Shelda seeks opportunities to use her gifts to benefit others. Her personality is sunny and infectious, and her smile is contagious. She is a member of Virtuous Women United and currently serves on the leadership team as Administrator and Secretary. Shelda loves to see people happy and fulfilled, and you will almost never catch her without a smile on her face.

To order autographed copies of this book please visit:
www.TheHeartThatSmiles.com

To order WHOLESALE copies of this book or others by College Boy Publishing, Call:
972-383-9234

Email:
collegeboypublishing@gmail.com

Or visit
WWW.COLLEGEBOYPUBLISHING.COM

www.ingramcontent.com/pod-product-compliance
Lightning Source LLC
Chambersburg PA
CBHW071208160426
43196CB00011B/2222